1984 Merry Christmas, Mildred

From Jennie

AMERICA
LAND OF WILDLIFE

by KAREN JENSEN
and the Editors of NWF Books

NATIONAL WILDLIFE FEDERATION

Library of Congress CIP Data: page 159

CONTENTS

Introduction

Imagine a nature-lover's paradise: a single country where you could find samplings of some of the world's most spectacular wildlife habitats. A country that would include rocky mountain ledges as rugged as some in the Himalayas; wind-swept grasslands as open and treeless as the Argentinian pampas; scorching deserts as dry and sandy as the Sahara; junglelike swamps as steamy as some in the Amazon. Well, if this sounds like an imaginary land, think again. The country is quite real. It is America.

We are often reminded of how many of America's wild places have been lost. Without question, through the years too much land has been taken from too much of our wildlife. Too many of our mountains have been overlogged and overmined; too many of our grasslands have been overgrazed; too many of our wetlands have been drained. However, thanks to the vision of many conservationists and thanks to the miraculous resiliency of nature, America is still a nation with a tremendous diversity of wildlife habitats.

That is what this book is about: It is a tribute to the astounding ecological variety within the continental United States. For we feel not only that our remaining natural heritage is worth protecting—it definitely is that—but also that it is very much worth celebrating. In that spirit, we offer you *America: Land of Wildlife*. We hope you enjoy it.

Land Among the Clouds:
THE MOUNTAINS

The making of the first mountain, a northeastern California Indian legend tells, began after Chareya created the world. He wanted to look upon the earth from his home in the sky, but the sky was too dark and the earth was very, very far away. Undaunted, Chareya set upon a solution. With his hands, he pulled open a hole in the sky, and through it he passed soil, sand, rocks, snow, and ice. The great mound grew and grew until it finally reached just a step below Chareya's home in the heavens. Now Chareya could easily visit the earth whenever he pleased, the legend goes. But it was on the mountain that he chose to dwell. And it was the mountain that served to link his two worlds: the earth and the sky.

Few would argue that America's mountains, with all their majesty and grandeur, make fitting homes for a god. But it is when they serve more earthly creatures that our mountains' true wonder emerges.

As a home for wildlife, a mountain's generosity cannot be matched, for a single mountain links not just two worlds, as Chareya's mountain did, but many. A given mountain, for example, can encompass a dry, warm desert world in its foothills and a cold, arctic world at its summit. In between, the mountain holds other treasures: an ouzel's crystalline stream; an elk's conifer forest; a black bear's berry-fringed meadow.

For some animals, even entire ranges bear gifts. A red-tailed hawk and its migrating brethren coast on the updrafts deflected along the Appalachians to ease the strain of the long, hard trip south.

Our mountains also become sanctuaries for creatures besieged by the encroaching hand of civilization. The fewer than 1,000 grizzlies remaining in the lower 48 make a last stand in the mountains of Wyoming and Montana. And the California condor, diminished almost to extinction, hangs on in the Sierras. Our mountains, as if aware of their eternity in the eyes of man, offer refuge to those whose days seem counted.

Highlighted by a quarter moon, Oregon's Mt. Hood rises into the night sky. The inhospitable, permanently snowy peak belies the rich and varied animal life on the lower slopes.

*"The tops of mountains are among the unfinished parts of the globe,
whither it is a slight insult to the gods to climb and pry into their secrets...."*

—Henry David Thoreau

Dusted by a winter snow-storm, the eastern face of the Sierra Nevadas juts abruptly from dry scrubland. In about two vertical miles, parts of John Muir's "Range of Light" rise from desert foothills to summits studded with alpine meadows— giving wildlife a variety of worlds to live in.

From the gentle contours of our eastern highlands to the stark ramparts of our western ranges, America's mountains rise from the earth in an impressive parade of different shapes and sizes.

There are high mountains and low mountains; mountains forested to the top and peaks permanently capped in snow and ice. There are rounded ridges in the Blue Ridge and jagged, saw-toothed crests in the Rockies; there are low, dome-shaped mountains in Utah and lofty, needle-peaked cones in the Cascades. Every range, every peak, reaches to the sky with its own character, spreading an endless bounty of food and shelter for the wildlife living on its slopes.

This rugged individualism is molded by the action of two mighty forces: One, rooted deep in the earth, thrusts mountains skyward; the other, working from the outside, sculpts and flattens mountains through time.

Consider the creation of the western ranges. The Rockies, Cascades, Sierras, and Pacific Coast Ranges are souvenirs of an upheaval that peaked some 60 million years ago. In some places, immense pressures deep within the earth wrinkled its crust to look like a rumpled blanket. In others, great blocks of rock faulted upward. Still elsewhere, volcanoes spewed molten rock. But the violence that created these tilted, tortured rocks tells only half their story. These mountains' spectacularly sculpted faces are also the result of the other powerful mountain-making force: erosion.

Untamed by the slow wasting of erosion, young mountains like Colorado's Maroon Bells (left) offer ragged peaks for the likes of mountain goats and tiny pikas. Time-worn ranges like the Blue Ridge Mountains in Virginia (right) provide forested ridges and valleys where deer and black bear find abundant food and shelter.

The gentle, rolling Appalachians in the East are proof that erosion is a force capable of moving mountains, for these forested ridges once may have been as steep and rugged as the high mountains out West.

The reason for the difference is, simply, age. Like sections of the western ranges, the Appalachians were created when portions of the earth's crust were pushed upward in massive, curved folds. But this transformation occurred almost 200 million years before the western ranges were raised, giving erosion that much longer to eat away at these venerable mountain veterans. Viewed with this vast scope of vision that geology imparts, the mighty Rockies are mere youngsters which, given time, may resemble the low, rolling Appalachians. And the Appalachians, ephemeral creatures that all mountains are, may be flattened into oblivion by the persistent hand of erosion.

Still, sculpting and leveling mountains remains an awesome task. To carry out its bidding, erosion marshalls the services of relentless agents. Chief among them is water—preeminent carver of mountains.

For it is water—frozen water—that has made the greatest changes upon the face of the earth. Up until their most recent retreat about 10,000 years ago, glaciers, great rivers of ice, scoured the countryside, taking huge bites out of the land. The ice at the front of a glacier shattered the rock beneath it into house-sized boulders and smaller, jagged pieces. As the great, weighty ice sheet moved—sometimes at speeds of more than 300 feet in a day—the glacier dragged the rock chunks, scarring the land along its path. Mountains worked over by glaciers, such as the Grand Tetons in Wyoming, show characteristic wounds: saw-toothed ridges; scooped-out basins; deep, U-shaped valleys.

Even today, water persists as erosion's most powerful mountain sculptor. Although most of the massive ice sheets of old are gone now, vestigial glaciers still grind some of the highest peaks in the West. A much more pervasive destruction occurs when water, even drop-

Mountains seem eternal, but they change constantly. Rivers like the Yellowstone (far left) carve deep canyons into their slopes. Tiny lichens (near left) secrete an acid that crumbles their rock. And roots of trees like bristlecone pines (below) wedge themselves into crevices, prying the stone farther apart.

lets, seeps into rock crevices and freezes and expands, splintering rock into boulders and smaller pieces. And gushing, flowing water does its share of spectacular mountain shaping. As it thunders down a mountain slope, a high-born torrent pounds its course with the debris it transports downhill. Through the years it will carve a deep cleft along its path, which in time may become a beautiful mountain valley.

Not all eroders are so obvious, however. Some of these forces are much more subtle, moving slowly, almost imperceptibly, to accomplish feats that a hastier force couldn't. Lichens—actually two ancient forms of plant, a fungus and an alga, bonded in a symbiotic relationship—are one such subtle force. True mountain pioneers, lichens are the first plants to invade barren rock, and they eat away at their hosts with primitive persistence. Lichens absorb tremendous amounts of water—more than 300 percent of their dry weight in some species. As the plant absorbs water, it expands, shattering slivers of rock. And the fungus secretes an acid which disintegrates the rock surface. Flake by flake, a minute pile of rock particles accumulates.

This slow chipping away at the mountain, however, does much more than turn mountains into molehills. The byproduct of this breakdown is life-sustaining soil. In time, enough rocky debris might accumulate around the lichen for a moss to settle there, further crumbling the tiny mound and adding organic matter to it. Eventually, enough soil might build up to support a hardy tree whose roots might grow into rock fissures and pry them wider open.

Working hand in hand, the forces that uplift mountains and the forces that wear them down give us the varied and spectacular scenery that makes America's mountains such special and awe-inspiring places. To the wildlife of the mountains, however, the gift is much more vital, for in creating a varied landscape, the mountain-making forces create a wealth of worlds where animals can play out their lives.

A glacier-gouged, sheer rock face becomes a place where bighorn sheep can scramble and retreat from less-nimble predators. The soil created by erosion becomes the life-sustaining matrix without which plants cannot grow, deer cannot forage, eagles cannot perch and build nests. But it is a mountain's height—a legacy of the forces that thrust mountains skyward—that makes a mountain an unparalleled home for wildlife.

As it rises, a mountain pierces through increasingly colder temperatures—about three degrees for every thousand feet of altitude. A single western mountain, for example, can embrace habitats ranging from the benign shelter of the piñon jay's forest in the foothills to a ptarmigan's cold, alpine kingdom at the summit. Even a cursory look at this layering of life, however, reveals a simple truth: It's not easy at the top.

Crowning most western mountains and a few scattered peaks in New England is one of the harshest mountain worlds of all—the alpine tundra. Approached from below, from the shelter of the coniferous forest, the alpine tundra's aura is felt long before this world is seen. With each step up, the air gets colder and the wind howls more fiercely. Soon enough, the forest begins to thin. Finally, only a few isolated trees stand sternly in battle against the cold, the wind, and desiccation. Some stand upright, but grow branches only on their leeward side; some are so gnarled and deformed that they seem to grow horizontally. This is the timberline, the highest forest frontier in the mountains. And this tattered and twisted line of trees is a fitting gateway for the harsh world just above.

Nature, as if to prove that only the hardiest of life deserves to live on its mountaintops, made the alpine tundra one of the most taxing environments on earth. The odds here appear stacked against survival.

At these high altitudes, winter only grudgingly releases its icy hold, lingering for up to eight frigid months. The air at these heights holds little heat, so the

temperature remains below freezing for five months, and even in summer seldom climbs above 60 degrees. Snowstorms can blanket the mountaintop any day of the year. High-speed winds are also a daily plight, often whipping at velocities of more than 100 miles an hour and drying everything in their path. The growing season is short: Spring is virtually nonexistent; summer, barely two months long. Making it even more difficult for plants to grow here, what soil there is generally is thin, porous, and unstable. The slopes are also usually steep, prone to rockslides in summer and avalanches in winter. Yet, despite its long list of severe conditions, the alpine tundra is not a barren wasteland.

Life holds its own in this never-summer land. Plants, thanks to some remarkable strategies, grow here, splashing the tundra in brilliant colors and delicate blossoms during the brief growing season. More amazingly, a few animals—who have the mobility to migrate downslope during the harshest times—live here year round. For these hardy creatures, such as the pika and the mountain goat, the harshness of the alpine tundra has an invaluable payoff: sanctuary from enemies during the long winter months.

The scale of plant life atop a mountain may surprise a first-time visitor, for here, where peaks soar to majestic heights, everything is low. Plants hug the ground or huddle next to a rock for protection. Life in the tundra looks beaten, but its low stance is, in fact, evidence of its victory. By growing close to the ground, alpine plants gain a double advantage. The wind is considerably slower close to the ground, so the plant is protected from the worst of the wind's chill and desiccation. In addition, the ground retains some of the sun's warmth, and the plant can draw from it. But sometimes, hugging

17

Cuddly baby mountain goats are tougher than they look. Born in the spring in high crags, they begin to climb and bound among the rocks almost immediately. Mama stays close by, though, with a sharp eye out for hungry eagles.

18

the ground is not enough to fend off the harsh conditions of the tundra.

Cushion plants add shape to low stance. They grow in a rosette which exposes a flat surface to the wind, but the greatest possible surface to the warmth of the sun. The tightly matted foliage also retains heat better than other growth patterns during freezing temperatures.

Many alpine plants also have extensive root systems to anchor them in the unstable soil and long taproots to reach the deep water supply. Brilliant blossoms help, too: Bright blossoms absorb more heat than pale ones, helping to keep the plant warm. But for most plants, one of the greatest hardships in the alpine tundra is the extremely short growing season. To cope with it, most plants here are perennials, and most are slow growers—a plant may take ten years to mature, and a plant six inches in diameter may well be 100 years old.

If diminutive size and vivid coloration are necessary survival strategies in the tundra, the mountain goat has broken both rules. About the size of a white-tailed buck and cloaked in a shaggy, white coat, this relative of antelope and sheep rules supreme on rocky cliffs for the entire year. The white coat has a double layer of fur which effectively shrugs off the freezing temperatures and the wind's chill. And it does more. The alpine air, which holds such little heat, also filters out little of the burning rays of the sun. The white coat of the mountain goat helps reflect those damaging rays. This king of the mountain even seems to use some of the harsh conditions to its own advantage. During the dead of winter, it seeks rocky slopes swept clean of snow by the howling winds and browses on twigs, shrubs, even lichens. When the wind has not laid bare its dinner plate, the mountain goat exposes a meal by pawing through the snow with its powerful legs.

The mountain goat's legs are perhaps its best equipment for negotiating sheer rock faces, for in this precarious world, sure footing is as essential for survival as food and water. Flexible, two-part hooves with textured pads give the animal a sure grip on rocky ledges. Short, stocky legs help improve the animal's balance.

Few things, in fact, seem to threaten the mountain goat in its kingdom near the clouds—not predators, not wind, not cold. But there is a danger on these steep cliffs that not even a sure-footed mountain goat can conquer: avalanches. Every year, the mountain's white death claims a few white knights.

On the mountain tops, the persistent force of erosion works with particular violence. Avalanches and rockslides steadily tame the mountain. Boulder by boulder, slab by slab, the rocky cliffs give way. Fragments broken loose slide or roll downhill until they come to rest on more level ground. Seemingly inhospitable, this pile of rocks, known as a talus rockslide, is home for another one of the select few mammals that live in the alpine tundra year round: the pika.

The pika, a hamster-sized relative of the rabbit, is well designed to keep warm. Its long, dense fur and its spherical shape are ideal for heat retention. Furthermore, its short ears and legs expose little surface area to the cold and thus are unlikely to freeze. But, this efficient design is still not enough, and the pika must rely on the rockslide for its winter survival.

In the taxing climate of the alpine tundra, where the double plight of freezing temperatures and desiccation are a common occurrence, the air pockets within the talus rockslide retain both warmth and moisture. As the temperature and the humidity fluctuate from month to month and even from night to day, the pika moves up and down the rocky maze, seeking the right combination of warmth and moisture. Snow accumulated on the surface of the rockslide increases the insulation provided by the talus labyrinth. The pika's citadel is also an ideal warehouse for winter food. Since the pika does not hibernate, it must collect and dry large quantities of grass and other plants to see it through the winter.

Come the first warming days of spring, the pika ventures out of its home for increasingly longer periods.

Since the growing season is short, the pika does not have much time to collect its winter provisions of grasses, sedges, and flowering plants, so it harvests at a frenzied pace. Clipping a sedge here and a grass clump there, even climbing a few feet up nearby trees to collect twigs, the pika works indefatigably and ceaselessly. Each load is brought to a flat rock and stacked in a "haypile." The sun and the ever-present wind soon dry and cure it. The pile grows quickly, for pikas have been observed to bring in up to 15 loads of hay in the course of one hour. And the pile grows tall, sometimes reaching a height of two feet. Yet this frenzied stockpiling, so critical for surviving the adversities of winter, exposes the pika to a quick-moving peril.

As the temperatures of spring and summer climb to more benign levels, so do the pika's enemies—coyotes, bobcats, and foxes—ascend to its rockpile from the forest below. And eagles swoop down at it from the sky. The pika's grayish brown coat evens the odds somewhat, for the little alpine harvester blends with the rocks on which it moves. If danger comes too close, though, the pika lets out a shrill, high-pitched whistle. Having issued its warning, the pika disappears into its rockpile in a flash. The talus is a safe refuge from all enemies—all, that is, except the wily weasel.

Against this most feared of predators, the pika has little recourse. Weasels are fast, moving like furred lightning bolts as they go after a meal. Worse yet, the

The jumble of a mountain rockslide proves to be useful for a variety of living things. Alpine bluebells (far left) nestle from the wind in the lee of a boulder. A short-tailed weasel (left) uses the rocks as lookout posts when on the prowl for pikas. The pika (above) gathers food to store in its rocky den for winter.

21

lithe, slender weasel can pursue the pika through the pathways of its sanctuary. Perhaps only a better knowledge of the talus rockslide's blueprint gives the pika a slight edge over this consummate hunter.

Below the stark talus rockslide lies another world entirely. The alpine meadow, nurtured by the spring and summer melt of a nearby snowfield, spreads a thick carpet of grass dotted with brilliant wildflowers.

Lush plant growth, in turn, entices creatures great

A golden-mantled ground squirrel (top), a cougar (middle), and a snowberry checkerspot butterfly (bottom) may all congregate in high alpine meadows (left) during the few warm months that bless high peaks.

and small into the meadow. On a summer day, the fields hum with insects, and butterflies vie with alpine wildflowers in a spectacle of fragile beauty. Startled, a water pipit shoots skyward from its nest hidden in the thick, green growth, filling the air with excited song. Elsewhere, a flash of striped fur marks the passage of a ground squirrel, one of many small rodents who burrow in the meadow's moist soil, aerating the earth and further encouraging plant growth.

23

The succulent grasses draw large animals from their wooded hideaways. Emerging from the forest below, elk move into the sunlight, tails flicking nervously. Caution is a must, for prowling carnivores follow their prey to the meadow. In these wide open spaces, these hunters are quick to spot any sign of activity. As the sleek, well-muscled form of a mountain lion slips into the field, activity stills and the meadow creatures retreat to where they feel safest: the cool darkness of a burrow or the shady shelter of the nearby forest.

For most animals, mountain life means forest life, for it is here that a mountain's great bounty is held. From the dizzying network of branches in the canopy to the shady, muffled world that hugs the forest floor, mountain forests offer almost unlimited opportunities for food and shelter to the creatures that live there.

Forest cover on our mountains falls into two main categories. Coniferous forests cover the western mountains and the higher elevations of the eastern mountains. Green throughout the year, these forests of spruce, fir, and pine are adapted to grow in cooler, drier regions. And deciduous trees cover all but the highest slopes on the eastern mountains. Oaks, maples, and the other trees that live here thrive in more benign climates with plenty of rainfall. Because trees have adapted so well to different climatic conditions, almost all mountains are ensured a sheltering forest cover.

For deer, elk, and other large, warmblooded animals that must maintain their body temperature within a narrow range, the mountain forest provides a critical service. Especially at higher altitudes, where the seasonal swings of weather are great, the forest serves as a protective shelter from storms, as a warm shelter from cold, and as a cool shelter from heat.

In winter and fall, the trees and low vegetation slow down the wind's speed, robbing it of some of its chill. Even a few degrees difference between the interior of the forest and an open area can make the difference between life and death for large mammals.

In the summer, the forest affords protection from the temperature fluctuations between night and day. When the sun beats down during the day, the forest's canopy of branches filters out much of the heat, creating a cool haven. At night, when the warmth of the day dissipates into the air, the forest retains a cushion of warmer air—an advantage for animals spending the night in the open. Aside from the thermoregulating benefits of the forest as a whole, however, the trees serve forest wildlife

in specific ways. In few places is this more apparent than in the buzzing activity within the canopy.

Watching life in the canopy is like watching a film in fast motion. Birds flit from twig to twig with quick movements, and squirrels, in erratic high-speed stops and starts, scurry along larger branches. But this seemingly random, perpetual motion is actually the serious, and orderly, business of finding mates, building nests, defending territories, and collecting food.

In a conifer forest, most of the canopy traffic is made up of seed-eaters. A bird commonly seen hopping overhead is the pine grosbeak. This bird's conical beak is ideally designed to break open pine-cone scales and get at the nutritious seeds within. Red and Douglas' squirrels

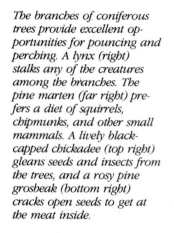

The branches of coniferous trees provide excellent opportunities for pouncing and perching. A lynx (right) stalks any of the creatures among the branches. The pine marten (far right) prefers a diet of squirrels, chipmunks, and other small mammals. A lively black-capped chickadee (top right) gleans seeds and insects from the trees, and a rosy pine grosbeak (bottom right) cracks open seeds to get at the meat inside.

An excellent climber, the pine marten can deftly pursue a squirrel to the highest of branches.

High on the branches, another pursuit is going on as the fraternity of insect-eating birds chases after meals. Chickadees, nuthatches, and assorted warblers glean the rich supply of insects that live on the branches and leaves and in the bark. In the course of gathering their meals, these birds serve their forest home well, for they help keep populations of tree-damaging pests in check. The supply of insects, however, disappears late in the year, and most insect-eaters leave the conifer forest in autumn in search of buzzing tidbits elsewhere.

Every trade has within its ranks a member that excels, and the insect-eating guild is no exception. The pileated woodpecker is so adept at finding insects that not even a winter shortage can stump it. It uses its sharp bill to drill into tree trunks, subsisting all season on the hidden insects, especially carpenter ants, that it extracts.

Like its prey, this bird also makes its home inside tree trunks. And although the pileated woodpecker is well-equipped to drill into hard, healthy wood, it often works on trees that have begun to die. Perhaps the tree was overcome by woodboring insects or disease; perhaps it was wounded by lightning during one of the mountain's thunderstorms. Perhaps it is simply an old-timer dying of old age. Whatever the cause, a weakened tree yields more easily to drilling than a healthy one, making the woodpecker's task easier.

In the wise economy of nature, dead and dying trees in the forest are not retired to a useless existence until they disappear—they simply change roles, acquire new tenants. The woodpecker's nest hole marks only an early use among many the dying tree will be put to through the years. Woodpeckers will occasionally occupy the same hole year after year, but generally they prefer to construct a new home for each new brood of eggs. And so, each season there are always some abandoned woodpecker holes for the taking, and no shortage of opportunists to colonize them.

also harvest cone seeds, but their methods are less refined. With its sharp teeth, the squirrel nips cones from the tree and lets them plummet. Then it descends to the ground, stashes some seeds in crevices, and takes others to the branches for a meal. Some seeds from the cache germinate to repopulate the forest with trees. The squirrel might have forgotten where it stashed some of the seeds, or perhaps the squirrel fell victim to an efficient predator and did not live to look for its cache.

The hordes of birds and squirrels drawn to the vast seed supply in turn attract predators that hope to make the harvesters into meals. A lynx may scramble up a tree to wait behind the veil of a branch for a likely meal. A pine marten might pursue its quarry more aggressively.

A hollow tree will be home, sweet home to wildlife families year after year. One year, a flying squirrel may peer from the cavity (far left); another, it might be a mother raccoon with two playful young ones (left).

29

The pair of large, dark eyes peering out from one such hole belongs to a flying squirrel, a tiny gray brown ball of fur whose ill-fitting suit billows and helps it glide from tree to tree. From its cozy, second-hand home, the flying squirrel makes forays into the forest to harvest a variety of foods in season; it stores acorns in the tree cavity as a hedge against lean times.

As the tree decays further and the wood becomes softer, other mammals can enlarge the hole and settle there to raise families. At this stage in the tree's life cycle, a female raccoon becomes a likely tenant. The enlarged tree cavity becomes a warm nest in which to bring a litter of young into the world. The loosened bark in the decaying tree also provides spaces where bats can roost.

Finally, the tree is so decayed, its wood so soft, that even a mild wind will break off its top. The tree's craggy remnant, called a snag, then becomes an ideal nest site for owls, who bring up their young in the hollowed-out depression at the top. Smaller birds such as chickadees and nuthatches can now excavate their own nests in the softened wood. Sadly, in most of our managed forests, snags are the exception rather than the rule, and some cavity nesters are hard pressed to find suitable homes.

The eastern bluebird, once a fairly common sight in low forest clearings, has in recent decades found that its natural nesting sites at the edges of forests have either disappeared or been taken over by more aggressive birds. Today, the sight of a bluebird is an uncommon treat. A lucky glimpse of this bird might catch it perched in a bush, surveying the incessant activity below.

Here, between the canopy and the forest floor, another layer of mountain life bustles in shrubs and small trees. Low bushes lure birds downward with offerings of plump, ripe fruit; and, like a stepladder to loftier lifestyles, they lure floor-dwelling creatures upward.

Most fruit-eating birds lead migratory lives, following the path of ripening fruit. The cedar waxwing, for example, generally summers in the northern United States and moves more widely across the States in the winter.

Its quest for fresh stores of fruit, however, often makes its movements unpredictable. When the bird discovers fruit, a greedy orgy begins. Cedar waxwings have such a taste for this delicacy that they have been known to gorge on berries until they can't fly. They even feast on over-ripe fruit until they are drunk. A fruit diet also shapes the lifestyles of other birds, though not in the same heady way as the cedar waxwing's.

The fruit supplies of the phainopepla, a glossy gray bird whose name comes from the Greek word for "shining robe," enable the bird to lead a double life. The phainopepla nests in the desert in spring; but as its fruit source dwindles, the bird migrates to mountains in the Pacific Coast Ranges. There, replenished by an abundant supply of fruit, it nests a second time.

The scarlet tanager successfully scours the low shrubs for berries, as well as for insects and caterpillars. But birds do not live by food alone, and the tanager also uses the shrubs for romance. Only the male is, in fact, a

Between the tree branches and the ground, the underbrush fairly bustles with activity. A young barred owl (left) surveys the busy scene from its perch on a decaying snag as a bluebird (above) scouts for berries and insects. Even some reptiles, like this smooth green snake (right), sometimes climb bushes for sunning and hunting.

scarlet bird, a feature the female apparently finds alluring. When the male courts, he stands on a low bush and spreads his black wings, revealing his scarlet back to the female watching overhead.

Coiled among the tangle of vines that loop and sprawl just above grassy patches in upland woods throughout much of the country may be found the sinuous smooth green snake. This fifteen-inch beauty spends most of its time in the grass hunting insects, worms, and centipedes, but sometimes it climbs vines and brambles to lie motionless, virtually disappearing amid the foliage.

In late summer, the female snake scouts for a suitable nest site in a depression under a flat rock, where she lays about a dozen eggs. The sun-warmed rock helps incubate the eggs, and within three weeks the eggs hatch and the young emerge into a mountain setting of small scale and intimacy: the forest floor.

As home for some of the mountain forest's smallest residents, the forest floor is a miniature land of enchantment. Seen from their Lilliputian vantage point, a fallen log becomes a bridge, an arched gateway, and a warm home. The layer of leaves on the ground is a hiding place, a nest liner, a colorful carpet. But magic is not restricted to the imagination in this kingdom, for here, a remarkable process of self-perpetuation goes on.

Fallen, decaying leaves add organic matter to the rich mountain soil. And the well-used tree, having crashed to the forest floor, enters the final stage of its existence. Bacteria and fungi work at the rotting wood, decomposing it. In time, the decomposed tree becomes part of the soil, where it serves as food for the forest's living trees. Earthworms churn the earth, working the mulch into the deeper layers of the soil. From the time a tree falls to the time it becomes new soil, however, many years must go by. In between, the fallen log serves many purposes to many animals.

When a tree first falls, perhaps toppled by lightning or a windstorm, it lies off the ground, supported by its branches. At this time, the top of the log becomes a

On the forest floor, death leads to life. A fallen tree and leaves (far left) deteriorate with the help of insects and mushrooms (left). Once broken down, they enrich the soil and nourish the plants that produce food for many creatures, such as these cautious deer mice (below).

kitchen counter for goshawks and other raptors as they stop there to pluck fur or feathers from prey. For ruffed grouse, the raptor's countertop becomes a staging area for their romantic strutting. Grouse may also nest in the space between the log and the ground, and snowshoe hares may also bring up their families in its warm protection. Even the exposed roots provide special services, as birds perch, dust, and even nest there.

As the log further decomposes and its bottom merges with the ground, deer mice build runways along the sides of and underneath the log. During the day, these little mice stay hidden in the privacy of their burrows. As the sun sets, they emerge to feed on berries and insects. Scurrying about from cover to cover like tiny children playing "war," the deer mice try their best to maintain low profiles. However, even under the cloak of darkness, the deer mice are not safe from the talons of night-hunting owls. In fact, deer mice often become meals for forest predators; their numbers are not endangered simply because they are such prodigious breeders, producing as many as eight litters a year.

Voles and shrews share the decaying log with the deer mice, burrowing through its core. These burrows become, in turn, homes and pathways for toads, skinks, and snakes, for the rotting log is always moist within.

Finally, as the log turns completely soft and lies almost buried in soil and forest debris, tree squirrels stash nuts in it, and voles feed off the fungi growing on it.

Within the borders of the mountain forest, a patchwork of clearings mingles with the stands of trees. These open areas, bathed in light, are centers of a tremendous amount of wildlife activity, for they attract not only many forest denizens but also the creatures who live exclusively in grassy, brushy openings.

The main attractions here are the succulent grasses and shrubs. This abundant food source in the clearing attracts vegetarians from many walks of life. Rabbits wend their way through the clearing, nibbling on grass blades between hops, and meadow mice emerge from

In a fern-crowded clearing, a white-tailed doe pauses and cocks her ears, alert to the slightest rustle that might signal approaching danger.

Perched amid a cold mountain stream like the one to the right, an ouzel, or dipper, shakes water off its feathers (far right). It has just surfaced from a plunge to the bottom in pursuit of insect larvae. These birds of western mountains not only dive, but also walk and "fly" under water to get food.

their burrows in the clearing to mow down leaves and stems. Coyotes, tantalized by the quantity of rodents in the clearing, come to exercise some pest control. As they leap in the sunlight after the scurrying mice, voles, and ground squirrels, they seem to jump for the pure and simple joy of it. Deer and elk also emerge from the shade of the nearby forest to feed on the lush vegetation of the clearing. The clearing, however, offers these large ungulates an added benefit.

In a deciduous-forest clearing carpeted with tall ferns, a white-tailed doe moves tentatively on thin, graceful legs. Suddenly she stops and freezes, her large, dark eyes alert, her ears cupping sound carried on the wind. This time it's a false alarm; she moves on.

The doe's concern was less for herself than for her fawn, lying motionless and completely hidden in the tall ferns. Provided the cover is tall enough, these clearings provide ideal calving grounds for deer and elk; as the young grow a little older, the high vegetation can be used to conceal them while the mother forages nearby.

At the edge of another mountain clearing, a black bear feasts on a richly fruited blackberry bush. Having had enough, she turns in the direction of the forest, briefly looking back. Her two cubs follow.

With her two cubs gamboling at her heels, the mother bear comes to the edge of a mountain stream, rushing and icy cold. She dips a sharp-clawed paw beneath a rock and heaves it over, quickly trapping the fat frog underneath with her large, flat paw. A patient teacher, she gives her catch to her young, but will soon expect them to join in her efforts.

The cubs, however, seem more interested in watching another waterside visitor than in their dead frog. Upstream, a mink, its coat wet and glistening in the sunlight, glides out of the icy water with a fish clenched in its sharp teeth. Taking wary notice of the bears, the mink, a lithe creature related to the weasel, opts for the shelter of the forest and turns its back—though briefly—on the bounty of the mountain stream.

No matter what their natural wealth, all mountain streams have seemingly insignificant beginnings. Melting snow and glaciers, rain, underground springs, and seepage at mountain tops create tiny rivulets that trickle down the mountainside, first picking their way around rocks and plants but becoming more forceful as they join forces and gain momentum. Like mountains, mountain streams have a series of life stages. They are most torrential when still young and react in froth, rapids, and swirling pools to the underlying form of the mountain. Older streams, like older mountains, usually are much less dramatic. They meander in gentle bends and curves on level beds. Whatever their character, though, mountain waterways remain one of the mountain landscapes most utilized by wildlife. Few creatures, in fact, are immune to the attraction of these watery avenues' offerings of drink, food, and open spaces.

In the rushing mountain torrents of the West lives one of the most unusual of stream dwellers. A drab little gray

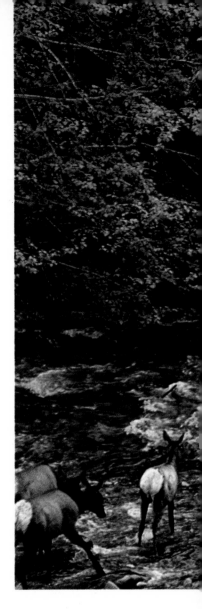

them warm. An extra-large oil gland helps keep them waterproof. Even their song is fitting of their lifestyle; it is clear and bubbly as a mountain stream.

Larger mountain streams carrying more water attract a different assemblage of water-loving animals, for these are the rivers of the true swimmers.

The river otter is so at home in the water that it seems a stranger in any other surrounding. With a torpedo-shaped body to cut efficiently through the water, webbed feet for propulsion, a thick tail for steering, and eyes and ears that seal when under water, the otter leaves no doubt as to its trade—fishing. Yet, while the otter is a dedicated and successful fisherman, its constant cavorting looks suspiciously enjoyable. There are many times, in fact, when one could swear that the otter moves just for the sheer fun of sliding, looping, and gliding through the fresh, clear water.

For some animals, the stream has an attraction beyond its sparkling water, beyond its thirst-quenching, food-giving attributes. Because a stream carves its way through dense forests, it becomes an open, winding pathway through woods that are tangled, even made impassable, by tree trunks and vegetation.

Large mammals such as elk and deer regularly use streams as pathways. During seasonal migrations to summer or winter grounds, when these animals travel in large herds, these avenues open a convenient route that many large bodies can follow. Especially after a harsh winter, when conserving energy during migration is critical, elk and deer can easily move along these watery trails to their summer destinations higher up the slopes. These routes also ensure that the animals have a steady supply of water from the stream and food from the lush vegetation growing on the banks.

We all dream about being architects of our own destiny. The beaver, enviably, comes closer to that dream than most other living things. Logger, architect, and engineer rolled up in one, this large rodent not only builds its own home but also alters its surroundings and

brown bird, the dipper, or water ouzel, revels in the frothy, icy water where it makes its home. John Muir's "hummingbird of blooming waters" stands on a boulder in the stream, bobs its body to some unknown rhythm, and then insouciantly walks into the water. As it searches for insects, snails, and immature fish, the dipper blithely walks completely underwater on the stream's bottom. This bird even "flies" through the water for short distances by flapping its wings.

Ouzels live along crystalline, high mountain streams throughout the year. They do not migrate in winter, and move farther down the mountainside only when their water source freezes. They build their nests on fallen trees or roots and on rocks and rocky ledges next to water, sometimes even under waterfalls. Some ouzels wash food before feeding it to their young.

Ouzels are well suited for so watery a life. They have membranes that close over their eyes and nostrils when they are under water, and plenty of down helps keep

Streams and rivers are important for more than drinking. Elk use them as expressways through tangled woods. The sprightly otter (left) fishes and frolics in them. And the beaver (right) dams them to make a home.

*A beaver's pond becomes the
site of its builder's lodge and
a growing place for plants
that attract the likes of
hungry moose.*

creates new worlds. Provided it has a stream, of course.

But give a beaver a stream, and the rest is history. First, the beaver builds a dam. The foundation usually is of mud and stones; then poles and brush are added. The assembly is then plastered with mud and soggy vegetation. Soon, water collects behind the dam and a deep pond forms. Then, in the center of the pond's deep water, the beaver builds its lodge.

The beaver constructs its lodge much as it builds the dam. By virtue of sitting in the middle of the deep pond and by having an entrance that can only be reached from under water, the lodge is a perfect retreat from terrestrial predators. Beavers even stash a winter's supply of food under water—the cold water helps keep cut shoots and branches fresh for winter feeding.

The new pond's still waters will now attract many new animals. Ducks, geese, and other waterfowl will come here to nest and raise their families. Some, like the moose, will find solace as well as food here. For this large mammal loves nothing more than to stand in a lake on a summer day, immersing itself in the coolness of the water and nipping pondweed and water lilies with its snout. The beaver creates a sanctuary for itself, builds a new habitat, and benefits its neighbors.

Mountains, too, are environmental architects, creating far-reaching new worlds. By acting as a barrier that robs rain-bearing air of its cargo, a mountain range helps form the dry lands of deserts and plains beyond it. By providing the raw materials for the making of soil, mountains give life to the lowlands. By serving as a birthplace of streams, mountains are also the mothers of rivers and all the life-sustaining marshes on their banks. Without mountains, in fact, our nation might not be the magical, diverse land we know.

Land of Endless Grass:
THE PRAIRIES

Ten million years ago, America's prairies were the scene of an amazing panorama. Rhinoceroses, elephants, camels, deer, horses, even giant bison grazed in a prairie of tall grasses. Since then, it seems almost unnecessary to say, the prairie has endured many changes, the most obvious of which is in its wildlife. After millions of years of evolutionary sorting and climatic upheavals, the wildlife of America's grasslands is smaller. All the huge mammals have disappeared forever, and the big ones that are left, the bison, in particular, live restrained lives in reduced habitats. Yet, despite those changes and the many differences between the prairie's current residents, a unifying thread connects all these creatures: All of them have been molded by life on open grasslands.

With a vast carpet of grass underfoot, the typical prairie animal is still a plant eater. It is also a swift runner or a skilled digger. The prairie is a vast open space with few places to hide from predators, and speed in running away or in plunging into burrows is the best means of escape. The product of the grasslands also has sharp vision, again because the prairie offers such vast vistas in which to see others or to be seen by them. And it is colored like the prairie, in the warm tan of dust in the sun. Of course, if an animal had all these characteristics, it would probably look stranger than one of its prehistoric kin. But most prairie animals embody at least two of these traits.

Like the life it supports, the prairie itself has seen much change, especially as American history has marched across it. But even in the wake of great change, there is something unchanging about the prairie. In the places where farms and ranches have replaced pure prairie, a persistent symmetry emerges as the prairie asserts its influence: Corn grows where tall grasses once waved, and cattle graze where bison once ruled. Man may tend it, but the land and the climate still have the final say about what plants and animals may live there.

A pronghorn grazes peacefully on the shortgrass prairie's open range. On the move, the pronghorn is the fastest North American mammal—sprinting at speeds of more than 50 miles an hour.

"Grass is the forgiveness of nature—her constant benediction....
Forests decay, harvests perish, flowers vanish, but grass is immortal."

—Senator John J. Ingalls

A muted rainbow and a rising moon at sunset mark the end of a prairie's stormy day. This land plays an indifferent host to many kinds of weather—blizzards, tornadoes, and hundred-degree-plus temperatures.

44

Once an unbroken sea of grass stretching some 600 miles east to west and over 1,000 miles north to south across the central United States, the prairie is now a patchwork quilt of ranches and farms, towns and cities, and bits and pieces of grassland. In its eastern portion—Illinois, Iowa, Minnesota, and Missouri—are remnants of the tallgrass prairie, or true prairie, where grasses sometimes eight feet tall grow thick with wildflowers and other vegetation on deep, fertile topsoil. In its western portion—in the Dakotas, Nebraska, Kansas, and Oklahoma—tall grasses merge with shorter grasses and form a transitional link to the westernmost grassland, the Great Plains. Also known as the shortgrass prairie, the Great Plains covers most of Montana, eastern Wyoming, Colorado, and New Mexico. Dry, even desertlike in places, it is characterized by short, resilient grasses that may reach only inches high.

As if refusing a stereotype, America's grasslands sport other guises as well. Surprisingly, one of the most extensive dune formations in the Western Hemisphere is a region of central Nebraska known as the Sand Hills. Covering nearly a quarter of the state, the Sand Hills were formed several thousand years ago when winds stripped the lightweight soil called "loess" from the sandy earth and left the sand to be whipped into dunes. Because of a good yearly rainfall, the Sand Hills are not desertlike at all, but are thick with green grasses and alive with the scratching of the small feet of rodents scurrying amidst the hooves of grazing cattle.

Remnants of a distant glacial past, large boulders and small pothole lakes dot northern portions of the verdant prairie.

In the western Dakotas, the Badlands are painted not with green, but with the earthy, sunset hues of weathered rock. Remnants of a highly eroded ancient prairie, the Badlands' bleak, rocky terrain offers little refuge except to nesting birds, among them cliff swallows, swifts, and rock wrens.

Water has transformed another part of the prairie, dotting the northern central states and parts of Canada with thousands of mirrorlike tiny lakes and marshes known as potholes. Important as nesting places for migrating waterfowl, they add to the prairie's bumper crops of corn and wheat yet another important yield: ducks. Although they are only a small portion of the nation's wetlands, prairie potholes are the birthplace for a tremendous number of waterfowl. Almost half of all North American ducks are born each year in potholes in the United States and Canada.

As diverse as these regions are, however, they do, nonetheless, have an underlying similarity—something that could be called, though quite unscientifically, the essence of prairie. Largely flat and treeless, America's grasslands are an area where the sky somehow seems larger, the horizon longer and lower. A lone human standing on a low, verdant hill feels at once insignificant yet omniscient as the world seems to begin at his feet and stretch its grassy arms out forever.

The source of this widespread similarity is something decidedly unprairielike: the Rocky Mountains. The story begins some 60 million years ago, when the Rockies were a new force dominating the landscape. Before that time, water-laden winds traveled unchecked from the Pacific Ocean across the Midwest, dropping rain on the thick forests that covered the flat plains. With the rise of the Rockies, the winds were forced upward.

The cool air at the high altitude caused the winds to release their moisture as they crossed the mountain range. The central flatlands beyond became drought-prone, and moisture-loving forests gave way to grasses.

Grasses like the foxtail barley (right) play David to the Goliath of prairie weather and fires. Supple, they bend instead of breaking when blasted by wind. And they can emerge phoenixlike only days after a burn.

Then, less than a million years ago, another powerful force shaped the developing grasslands. Glaciers from Canada invaded most of the Midwest, sweeping over the Dakotas, Minnesota, Wisconsin, Michigan, Illinois, Iowa, Nebraska, and into Missouri. As these great ice sheets scraped the land, they broke up rock into boulders and other finer fragments—transporting the load for hundreds of miles.

About 10,000 years ago, the climate warmed, and the ice retreated—leaving its legacy behind. In places, large boulders sat incongruously in the middle of flat fields. And all over the landscape, winds spread countless tons of light, fine-grained loess that had been scraped up by the glaciers and ground to powdery dust by the melting ice sheet. Highly permeable and hundreds of feet deep in places, this soil proved perfect for the growing of grasses. The American prairies had been born.

The establishment of the prairie was a once-in-history event, but its maintenance is never ending. Low rainfall

48

and rampant winds consort to maintain the prairie. The low precipitation and periodic drought starve trees to death, but merely cause grasses to become dormant. The high winds, which blow unrestricted across the prairie's great, flat distances, increase the dryness by hastening evaporation. And while wind merely ripples the flexible grasses like waves in the sea, its force stunts the growth of trees.

Weather in the prairie is unpredictable, often giving rise to sudden, violent storms. Blizzards sweep unrelentingly across the plains, covering feed and freezing animals. In former years, bison and pronghorn died by the thousands in these whiteouts.

The prairie has also proved a perfect caldron for cooking up another kind of storm. When warm air from the Gulf of Mexico collides with cool, dense air moving in from the northwest, the result is a violent thunderstorm or, if conditions are right, a tornado.

Tornadoes are more common in the American Midwest than anywhere else in the world. With the wind walls of their funnels spiraling at 300 miles per hour, the usually dark but sometimes misty white tornadoes travel over the ground at speeds from 25 to 60 miles per hour. A tornado, as if it were a child angered by being told to pick up his toys, can be tremendously destructive, dismantling houses and peeling up blacktopped roads. Even fish have been sucked out of streams or potholes. Generally, however, animals easily move out of the way of the short-lived funnel. And the prairie itself remains largely untouched. Its low profile shrugs storms off as easily as a cow shrugs flies off its back.

Prairie seasons are also prone to great temperature extremes. Although considered to have a temperate climate, the prairie may reach 113 degrees in summer and plunge to 45 degrees below zero in winter. Fierce blizzards that impede travel are also a common plight here. "There are places in North America that are colder than the prairie Midwest, and some that are hotter," says prairie scholar John Madson. "But I'll stack our prairie

country against any as the hottest cold place, or the coldest hot place, on the continent."

Grasses survive these extremes by changing themselves. Most lie dormant during the cold autumn and freezing winter. Many of those growing in the near-desert Great Plains also remain dormant in the summer, when the drought is at its worst. Their vast underground root systems allow them to survive drought by reaching deep below the surface to the only available water. And grasses are even designed to survive the munching of prairie dogs, pronghorn, and other efficient grazers of the prairie. Since grass leaves grow continuously from their bases where nibbling teeth don't reach, the grazer's mowing is like a beneficial pruning—the grasses grow back lush and juicy and the animals are ensured a perpetual pasture.

The vagaries of weather are joined by the threat of fire. Fire is so prevalent here that the Indians of the Michigan prairie had only one word, *sce-tay,* to name both prairie and flames. Started by lightning or a man-made spark and fueled by dry grasses, the fire roars through the prairie in 40-foot walls of flame that move with the wind, driving frightened wildlife before it.

To the animals of the prairie, fires are a fateful event.

Some birds and pronghorn outdistance the flames, but others panic and flee into the fire. Burrowing animals, though, are generally safe; temperatures reach hundreds of degrees overhead, but the burrows rise in temperature only a few degrees. However, much of prairie life—reptiles, small rodents with shallow tunnels, nestlings, and rabbits, for example—succumbs.

Grasses, in contrast, are rejuvenated by fire. Only days later they emerge phoenixlike, poking delicate green shoots through the blackened stubble. Because the fire burns off a thick thatch of dead grass that crowds out new grass, the earth-protected roots send up new shoots even thicker than before. Yet shrubs and young trees—highly vulnerable to flame—will have disappeared after the fire, having once again lost their meager foothold on the prairie. For thousands of years, fire has helped to maintain the prairie as an open grassland.

The beauty of the grasses adorning these open spaces is understated, but nonetheless, it is powerfully evocative. Grasses—which are pollinated by the wind—lack the flamboyant appeal, the scent, and the sweet nectar of insect-attracting flowers. Yet their thin, flexible stems bend gracefully in the wind without breaking, and their slender, arching leaf blades shine as they drink up the light from the unobstructed sun.

Nowhere is this beauty more apparent than in the tallgrass prairie. With the highest annual rainfall—20 to 25 inches—and most nurturing soil of the prairie regions, it boasts the most luxuriant and spectacular plant growth of the prairies.

Because deep, fertile topsoil is a major contributor to this luxuriant growth, most of the original tallgrass country has long been cultivated. Today, only about one percent of the original 400,000 square miles of tallgrass prairie remains. The largest single patch is a section of the Flint Hills in eastern Kansas.

Viewed from a high place, a tallgrass prairie can appear impenetrable and nearly solid. But step up close, part the grasses and walk through them, and the tallgrass prairie becomes another world entirely. Most arresting are the grasses themselves. In low, moist regions, big bluestem, king of the tallgrass prairie, prevails. With strong stems taller than a man, thick foliage with leaves two feet long, and a dense network of roots, it holds the land in so tight a grip that few other plants can grow in it. Another tall grass, Indian grass, is less domineering, yet may be more widely distributed throughout the tallgrass prairie. Slightly shorter than bluestem and Indian grass, coarse switch grass needs less moisture and so is often found on higher ground.

The grasses themselves are only part of the prairie spectacle. Amid the sheltering stems of the grasses are found thriving populations of rodents, insects, and

Tall enough in places to hide a standing human, the slender grasses of the tallgrass prairie (left) now rule over only patches of their former kingdom. Nevertheless, they still offer food and shelter to little creatures like these curious harvest mice (right).

birds. A faint rustle might give away the presence of harvest mice feeding on seeds; a flutter of wings, the abrupt departure of a meadowlark or bobolink.

And there are other treasures in the grasses. A procession of wildflowers blooms from spring through autumn, washing the fields in waves of different color each time a new batch blazes into bloom. Because they must compete with the grasses for sunlight, taller and taller flowers prevail as the season passes. By late summer, flowers no longer shyly peek through low grasses; the statuesque sunflower and hardy goldenrod greet a human viewer face to face.

By day and by night, the voices of the prairie can be exuberant and pervasive. Particularly so is the strident

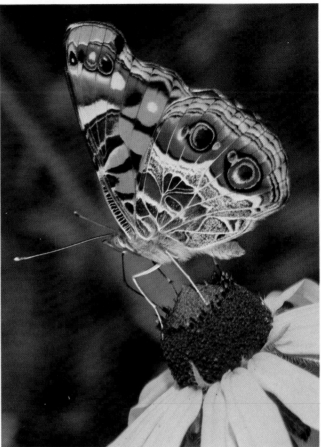

buzzing of the insects who are, quite simply, everywhere. It has been estimated that a single acre of tallgrass prairie in August harbors as many as ten million
insects. And rightly so. Insects are indispensable to
prairie life. Bees, butterflies, and moths pollinate the
prairie's wildflowers. Many of these and others also
serve as meals for the birds, small rodents, and even
other insects that inhabit the tallgrass prairie.

Among the most prevalent—and pesty—of the
prairie insects are the members of the grasshopper
family. Ubiquitous insects that they are, grasshoppers,
locusts, and crickets graze on every plant in their path.
Usually, insect-eating birds and cold, damp springtimes
keep their numbers in check; but in the 1870's, one

species—the Rocky Mountain locust—descended upon the prairies in unprecedented hordes. Arriving in glittering brown clouds, they left regions of the prairie barren and farmers' crops devastated. But they didn't harm most wildlife—mobile grazers merely moved to unaffected areas.

The locust invasion is an exception to a usually gracious mode of life in which prairie residents seem to accept the prairie's good graces and repay it with favors of their own. Such a trade-off is evident in a continuous exchange between prairie soil and the many creatures that burrow in it. The soil—soft and loose as far down as four feet below the surface—is perfect for digging and offers its residents protection from fire, climatic ex-

tremes, and predation. The burrowers, in turn, benefit the prairie by mixing up its soil, blending in nutrients, and aerating it so it can absorb water more rapidly.

So successful is this relationship that much of prairie life is conducted at the bases of the waving grasses or amidst the thick tangle of their roots. One among many burrowers, the prairie vole patters around the stems of the tall grasses and stores food in underground burrows. Another burrower, the industrious plains pocket gopher, can tunnel several hundred feet in one day and spends perhaps as much as 90 percent of its life under ground. The gopher, which takes its name from *gaufre,* the French word for its honeycomb of tunnels, has external fur-lined cheek pockets which it stuffs with seeds harvested from grasses and nuts gleaned from an occasional tree.

While these animals are safe from many predators when in their burrows, one enemy—the badger—is especially feared because it has all their tricks and more. The badger is a powerful animal which may weigh over twenty pounds. For all its bulk, however, it can rapidly dig itself into invisibility. Able to outdig the pocket gopher, the badger will pursue it through its home. It has been known to drag rabbits underground and stay put until hunger urges it to hunt again.

Above ground, life in the tallgrass prairie has a showier flair to it—especially among the birds. Unlike most forest birds, most prairie birds sing while in flight and have clear, lusty songs that easily fill vast spaces. But if their vibrant performances may appear to be intended for a large audience, in fact, they are usually intended for a very small and select one—a potential mate or an intruder into reserved territory.

One of the showiest birds is the prairie chicken, whose dramatic courtship ritual may have inspired several Plains Indian dances. The dances of the male prairie chicken begin in midwinter and continue until spring, increasing in frequency and, unless the performances are inadequate, culminating in mating.

The prairie is a good home—inside and out. Badgers (left) and other burrowing animals find the deep soil soft for digging and the root-laced sod perfect for strong ceilings to their tunnels. For prairie chickens, the open spaces are perfect for courtship, including settling disputes between jealous males (below).

In the hazy, pre-dawn hours, a handsome speckled male stalks into the middle of a prairie clearing and stamps the ground with his feet. With head lowered so that the head and neck feathers stand erect like an elaborate headdress, and with tail spread like a fan, the bird inflates orange sacs on his neck as he emits low, booming cries. Audible from even a mile away, his calls soon draw a collection of females, who mill about the borders of the dance grounds, as well as some potential male challengers. Fights frequently break out but are rarely harmful. Once they are resolved, the victorious male, perhaps joined by a few others, returns to his dancing and booming until the females in the audience have selected their mates.

While the hardy prairie chicken lives on the grasslands year round, most prairie birds are migratory and enliven the plains in seasonal waves of activity. The hub of most of this fluttering commotion is the prairie pothole region, about three million acres of the northern Midwest—principally in Minnesota, South Dakota, and North Dakota.

The prairie potholes were formed as glaciers carved hills and depressions in the landscape. When the great blocks of ice melted, the water filled the depressions. Scattered like bright jewels in the green fields of grain, they are replenished by rain and melting snow.

Although waterfowl fly in and out of the pothole region throughout late winter, summer, and fall, the most

Prairie potholes like the one above look insignificant, but because of their vast numbers they are critical breeding and nesting grounds for migrating waterfowl like the mallards at right. About half of all North American ducklings are born in the pothole region each year.

furious activity occurs each spring when the potholes serve as nesting sites for mallards, pintails, and about a dozen other species of ducks.

The potholes are an ideal nesting site for ducks because they offer the great number and variety of wetlands the nesting ducks seek. Although some of the potholes cover more than a hundred acres, the typical pothole is much smaller; as many as a hundred may be packed into a single square mile. Some are small marshes which hold snow melt and runoff for only a few weeks each spring.

Because ducks prefer to be isolated from others of their species when courting and nesting, they usually first take to the small marshes and surrounding grassy hills. When their young hatch, the ducks' needs change. Isolation is no longer necessary, but safety from predators is. The ducks and their young then move to the open water offered by the larger potholes and retreat to the thick marsh vegetation when threatened.

For many other birds, the potholes are not a nesting site, but a place to rest their wings and refuel for their long migrations. Flocks of snow geese, for one, arrive in mid-March and visit the potholes for only two weeks or so before making their way to their northern nesting grounds. And in fall, great flocks of Canada geese descend upon the prairie potholes en route to their southern wintering grounds. Like most migrating ducks and geese, Canadas prefer to fly at night, though when conditions are right they also will fly during the day. As they pass overhead, calling to each other in their distinctive honk, the hundreds of thousands of flapping wings create a soft roar and the striking V formation brands the face of the full moon.

When winter arrives, a strange calm settles over the potholes. Where recently the low depressions were alive with birds, they now are smothered with snow and ice. The air is emptier, no longer filled with the noisy, excited maneuvering of its feathered hordes. Even the lives of their year-round residents—among them wea-

Wings blurred, Canada geese prepare to land among the prairie potholes. The journey from their breeding grounds in Alaska and Canada to their southern wintering grounds is long and hard. The potholes are important stopovers that allow the birds to refuel and rest before continuing on their trip.

sels, raccoons, and skunks—and occasional visitors—fox and coyotes and, less frequently, a snowy owl descending from northern climes—seem to become muted by the snow. Throughout the long winter, the potholes remain a frozen, silent world—a sleeping goddess awaiting the kiss of early spring.

Just as the flow of water revivifies the pothole country in the spring, so it shapes all of the prairie's worlds. West of the lush tallgrass prairie, the land shows the effects of a gradually diminishing water supply. Closer to the rain-thirsty Rockies, the plant cover of the land changes. With it comes a new set of wildlife.

Annual rainfall in the Great Plains is only five to fifteen inches, some twenty inches a year less than in the tallgrass prairie. Consequently, its dominant plants are well adapted to drought. Buffalo grass, which grows only a few inches tall, has a twofold system for gathering water. Like the tall grasses, it sends long roots deep into the soil. It also has a network of fine roots that lie just beneath the surface and absorb rainfall as soon as it penetrates the surface. Like blue grama, another prevalent short grass, buffalo grass also sends off shoots above ground, helping to colonize the plains and keep its loose soil from eroding.

A taller grass, the two- to three-foot-high western wheatgrass, accomplishes this and more. Because it has underground shoots, its buds may survive even when drought kills the parent plant. To fight water loss when water is at a premium, the plant's dark-green leaves curl up to decrease the surface exposed to the drying air.

Another plant, needle-and-thread grass, has found an innovative way of outwitting the wind and securing a hold for its offspring on the Great Plains ground. Each of its pointed seeds has a slender, threadlike arm called an awn. Twisted when dry, the awn straightens when rain wets it and then twists again as it dries, screwing the seed into the earth.

Just as this stubborn hold on the soil typifies most plains grasses, it also characterizes the best-known plains resident: the prairie dog. With its intricate underground towns, the prairie dog links seemingly unconnected plains plants and animals in an invisible web.

The prairie dog is an excellent architect and earth mover. Working with nothing but the dry plains soil and its own strong legs, it constructs a spacious underground apartment that meets all the requirements for its family's comfort and safety.

Although no two are alike, and although they may vary tremendously in size, prairie dog burrows all tend to have certain features in common. The large mound at the main entrance, typically one to two feet high and five to ten feet wide, keeps out runoff from rain and serves as an observation post for the ever-vigilant prairie dog. In-

Sociable prairie dogs (right and below) dig tunnel towns in the shortgrass prairie. Their constant digging aerates the earth and brings new soil to the top, where it becomes a seedbed for replenishing the grasses that are a boon to grazing bison.

The stoop of a prairie falcon sends a squealing prairie dog toward the sanctuary of its burrow (above). But the sanctuary is not honored by all: Lithe black-footed ferrets (top right), now an endangered species, pursue the dogs through the maze of tunnels. And squatters like these burrowing owls (bottom right) freeload in the dog's abandoned burrows.

side the entrance, a listening room is constructed near the surface. Here, the prairie dog waits out threats of danger. The main tunnel, which may extend for dozens of feet more, links sleeping chambers, a grass-lined nursery, and a separate room used as a toilet. Another special feature, a room slanted upward, helps keep the prairie dog from being drowned in its home by providing an air pocket in case of flooding.

On a warm spring day, a prairie-dog town bustles with activity. At the entrance of one burrow, a tawny head appears. The prairie dog, a little over a foot tall when sitting on its haunches, surveys the scene and then scampers out, greeting an acquaintance with a quick "kiss." Elsewhere, a mother grooms her young while other pups roll and tumble in a playful fight, filling the air with a shower of high-pitched shreaks. Many prairie dogs feed on the grasses near their burrows, sitting up on plump haunches and keeping a watchful eye for danger while they nibble. Others, flattened on the soil, drink up the early morning sunlight.

Suddenly, one watchful prairie dog utters a series of two-part, high-pitched cries. In an instant, dozens of heads are raised and, as the shadow of a falcon sweeps over the ground, the entire population dives into

burrows. Above ground, the prairie-dog town lies still and empty; below, its creatures wait for the large bird to glide out of sight.

Danger is always present in a prairie-dog town, for the animals have many predators which may approach from almost anywhere. Besides the large predatory birds which swoop from the sky, there are many predators to fear on the ground. Burrowing owls, which sometimes make their homes in prairie-dog burrows, have a taste for their hosts and will scoop up young pups. Roaming coyotes, bobcats, and foxes also pounce on stray prairie dogs who can't reach their burrows in time. And the danger continues below ground; rattlesnakes and bullsnakes slither down burrows both to escape the daytime heat and in search of hiding prey.

Another especially feared predator combines the snakes' sinuous moves with a cunning directed almost exclusively at the killing of prairie dogs. This is the black-footed ferret, a member of the weasel family. The ferret, a lithe, masked hunter that lives and travels in prairie-dog towns and subsists almost entirely on prairie-dog meat, pursues the animals through their burrows. Prairie dogs may attempt to stop such invasions by blocking the passageways of their burrows with plugs of dirt, but the effort is rarely successful.

As a species, however, it is the black-footed ferret who is suffering. Possibly never large in numbers, the ferret is now believed to be the rarest of North American mammals, an unfortunate byproduct of persistent efforts to exterminate prairie dogs.

Prairie-dog towns once covered great patches of the plains. In the nineteenth century, a single prairie-dog town riddled a 25,000-square-mile patch of Texas and was thought to contain 400 million animals. But because ranchers believed the animals deprived grazing cattle of grass and because prairie dog burrows were hazards for horses and livestock, a massive campaign to poison prairie dogs began. Today, most prairie dogs live on protected lands and their towns are much smaller; one covering 200 acres is considered extremely large.

Far from disturbing the natural plains, however, prairie-dog towns greatly enhance it. Like the tallgrass's burrowers, the prairie dog helps improve the soil with its digging. Fresh soil brought to the surface encourages new plant growth, which in turn draws a great influx of life to the plains. Large and small grazers come to nibble on the new growth. Insects dart about the flowers and grasses, attracting birds. Attracted by the abundant food supply and the temporary shelter offered by the prairie-dog burrows, many small animals—mice, cottontails, jackrabbits, ground squirrels—also move into the area. These small creatures in turn attract a host of larger predators such as watchful owls from the sky and

prowling coyotes from the surrounding hills.

An intricate natural balance allows many of the plains' residents to exist peacefully side by side. Three Great-Plains classics, for example—the pronghorn, the bison, and the prairie dog—rarely disturb each other although they often graze within sight of each other in the same grassy terrain. Because each favors a different kind of vegetation, they don't compete for food. In fact, each one's habits generally benefit the other animals. By closely cropping the grass near a prairie dog's burrow, the bison increases the prairie dog's range of vision, making its watch for enemies somewhat easier. And by digging up lots of loose dirt, the prairie dog creates a dust bath for the bison, who rolls in the dust to rid its shaggy coat of pesky insects. The only time animosity is likely to result is when a pronghorn or bison tramples a prairie dog's mound. Then, the little animal will erupt in a fury of high-pitched insults before it dutifully sets about rebuilding its home.

Plains life does involve tremendous hardships, however, and summer's droughts and winter's blizzards regularly take their toll, sturdy and adaptable though plains animals are. Yet their greatest test of survival has come not from fierce weather or other natural events, but from human intervention.

One seasoned survivor is the coyote. Long despised as a pest and predator of farm animals, the cunning coyote has met man's determined extermination efforts head-on. And it is winning. Through its adaptable diet, keen intelligence, and large litters, it has actually expanded its range. A scruffy animal about the size of a medium-large dog, it usually eats small rodents, although when it hunts in packs it may add larger fare, such as the pronghorn, to its diet.

The pronghorn, neither an antelope nor a deer, combines qualities of both. Native only to North America, the graceful chestnut-and-white creature is a quintessential plains animal. Keen of eyesight and fleet of

The coyote (left) and the snowy owl (right) sometimes share the prairie's winter supply of food. The coyote is a permanent resident, but the snowy owl dips down into the American grasslands only in lean years, when its food supply dwindles in its northern home.

The bison, a symbol of America's grasslands, usually shrugs off the prairie's frigid winters. Warmed by its thick coat, it plows through snow with its head to reach nourishing grasses underneath.

foot, it races over the plains at forty miles per hour, occasionally sprinting at up to fifty miles per hour and easily beating any predator in sheer speed. Yet, by the early 1900's, only 13,000 pronghorn remained; they could not outdistance their popularity as a game animal or survive the constant reduction of their range. While today's plains contain over half a million pronghorn, these herds would be dwarfed by the numbers of those of old, which were second in size only to those of that symbol of open spaces, the bison.

The bison's numbers in the days before the prairie and plains were settled are legendary. In 1871, Major Richard I. Dodge, while crossing the Arkansas plain, saw a huge, thundering herd that was "about five days passing to a given point, and not less than fifty miles deep. From the top of Pawnee Rock I could see from six to ten miles in every direction. The whole space was covered with buffaloes...."

There were probably over 50 million of the shaggy beasts roaming North America around Dodge's time; about 50,000 now live in protected herds. Once slaughtered to the brink of extinction, they live today in a peace usually broken only by the bison themselves. During mating season, the huge males grow aggressive and charge at each other, their massive heads clashing. For the rest of the year, they live on the outskirts of groups of females quietly grazing on land their ancestors once dominated. Like the prairies and plains, their far roaming ways have changed, but they have endured.

Land of Little Rain:
THE DESERTS

Desolation Canyon, Furnace Creek, Buzzard Gulch, Arsenic Spring, Ruin Park, Dead Horse Point, Poison Strip, Bitter Springs, Devil's Backbone, Hell Hole Canyon, Starvation Creek, Funeral Mountains, Land's End: These names do more than tally places; they describe an attitude, a perception of America's deserts.

In Arizona's Cabeza Prieta Mountains, spiny chollas and stately organ pipe cacti thrive in the parched heat of the Sonoran Desert.

Yet the prospectors and settlers who saw the desert as a place of death cannot be blamed for what may seem a narrowness of vision. Their reaction is largely an inescapable one of their species: Man is not a desert animal. He cannot survive in the desert without a great deal of special preparation. A prospector without water had little chance of surviving more than a couple of days in 110-degree temperatures.

But, as in some scrappy marriages, conditions in the desert seem deadly only to the eyes of outsiders. To those nature has equipped to inhabit it, the desert supplies an ample larder. To be sure, the desert's arid clime creates a challenging environment. Desert animals display some of the most specialized adaptations of any of America's wildlife. Desert plants, too, are a special lot: a group of strange forms with strange life cycles not commonly seen elsewhere.

America's deserts are, in fact, havens of an unexpectedly rich variety of animal life. Yet it is the nature of the desert that much of this life is hidden. It is not much noticed by travelers because part of its survival tactic, like that of all animals, is to seek out optimal conditions for browsing, hunting, digging—for surviving. In the desert, that means much activity is conducted beyond the reach of the blistering heat: underground and under the cool umbrella of night.

There is, however, at least one desert name that comes unwittingly close to capturing this secretive quality of the desert. A weathered plaque near a uranium mine in the Utah desert reads—*Hidden Splendor.*

"...there are true secrets in the desert. In the war of sun and dryness against living things, life has its secrets of survival....Life could not change the sun or water the desert, so it changed itself."

—John Steinbeck

Fashioned by the desert's heat and winds, rippling dunes spread like a carpet of sand in Monument Valley, Arizona. This constantly shifting environment excludes all but the hardiest and most well-adapted plants and animals.

America's deserts are never short on surprise. Ranging from snow-covered mountains to flower-studded fields, they present an amazing and unexpected variety of scenery. Of course, America's deserts also include the stereotypical prospect of sand-swept slopes, cacti, and darting lizards. But this is only one facet of what is, in fact, the greatest assortment of desert types in any one region of the world.

All of America's deserts lie in an immense region that includes much of the Southwest and reaches northward into Oregon, Idaho, and Wyoming. To the west of the deserts jut the Sierra Nevadas and the Cascades. To the east rise the Rocky Mountains. In this region, America's five distinct deserts—the Great Basin, Painted, Mojave, Sonoran, and Chihuahuan—fall into one of two larger groupings: the northern, or cold, deserts and the southern, or hot, deserts.

The northern deserts include the Great Basin and the Painted Desert. America's largest, the 200,000-square-mile Great Basin Desert covers most of Nevada, Utah, southeastern Oregon, southern Idaho, and southwestern Wyoming. An appendage of the Great Basin, the Painted Desert covers southeastern Utah and northeastern Arizona as well as chunks of Colorado and New Mexico. Wetter than the southern deserts, with up to ten inches of precipitation a year, these northern deserts are much cooler, too, and hence have earned the seemingly contradictory name of cold desert.

The three southern deserts are the Mojave, Sonoran, and Chihuahuan. Situated in southern Nevada and southeastern California, the Mojave is home of the infamously brutal Death Valley, possibly the hottest place on earth. The creatures and plants living there must cope with temperatures as high as 134 degrees, the highest ever recorded in the United States. The Sonoran Desert in the United States fills the southeastern tip of California and most of southern Arizona with the classic desert beauty of rocky plains and towering cacti. The Chihuahuan Desert is America's southernmost desert. It

lies mostly within the Mexican state of Chihuahua, but it invades southwestern Texas and New Mexico. All three deserts receive very little rainfall—usually no more than five inches a year, and often less—and are warm in winter and searing hot in summer.

The northern and southern deserts are differentiated not just by temperature and rainfall, but also by patterns of plant and animal life. Low grasses and shrubs in the north give way to cacti and tall shrubs and trees in the south. Pronghorns and sage grouse in the north yield to piglike peccaries and cactus wrens in the south.

But these groupings are not rigid: two of the cold deserts find common ground with one of the hot deserts. Much of the Great Basin, Painted, and Mojave Deserts are characterized by stark mountains and the flat plains—or basins—that link them. The Great Basin is named not for one basin but for a series of basins partly filled with deep beds of sediment that rains washed down from the desert's highly eroded mountain ranges. Because most of the basins do not have drainage outlets, a heavy rainfall transforms portions of them into temporary lakes. The glaring sun usually evaporates these lakes in short shrift, however, and more often than not they exist as dry salt flats, called *playas,* largely devoid of life and glitteringly bright in the desert sun.

With little vegetation to hold the soil in place, water does much landscape carving in the desert. Rain flashes over the naked mountains, roiling huge amounts of soil, sediment, and rocks downhill into fan-shaped deposits on the desert floor. Water has carved the rock of the Painted Desert into mesas and canyons and shaped such marvels as the Sipapu natural bridge in southeastern Utah and the 1000-foot-high pillars of red sandstone in Arizona's Monument Valley.

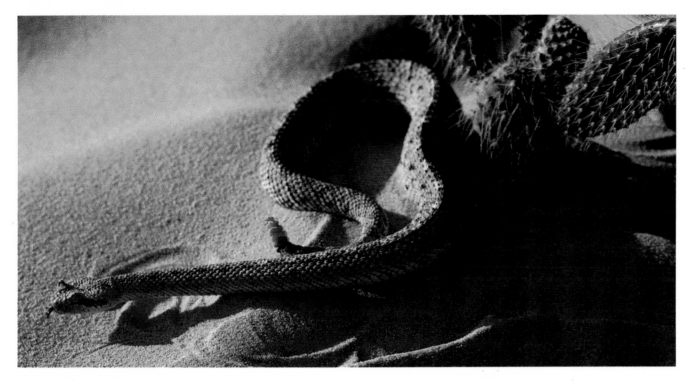

Two animals of the shifting desert sand dunes greet the day in different ways. At sunrise the desert rattler (left) will seek cool shade, but the horned lizard (below) will pop out of its nighttime sand shelter to warm up.

Another of the desert's facets, the sand dunes are the joint creation of the wind and obstacles in the wind's path. The winds blow sand from mountains and buttes, and the obstacles—low bushes, perhaps, or rocky ledges—block the path of the blowing sand, causing dunes to form.

Dunes are scattered throughout America's deserts. Northern Nevada and southern Colorado have large sand dunes. Dunes create streamlined slopes on the western edge of Death Valley. They appear like unmelting snow banks in the White Sands region at the northern border of the Chihuahuan Desert in New Mexico. America's largest range of dunes is the Algodones near Yuma, Arizona. Stretching in a sinuous chain fifty miles long, these dunes are five miles wide and up to 300 feet high. The tallest dune in America reaches 470 feet into the sky above southern Idaho.

The shifting sand of dunes makes life impossible for plants and animals not specially adapted for so loose and movable a terrain. Yet long-rooted plants do take hold, and in early morning hours the dunes often show evidence of other residents as the tiny footprints of insects, mice, and lizards and the smooth signatures of snakes speak of bustling nighttime activity.

Diverse as the deserts' many features are, one characteristic links them all: dryness. Yet while this characteristic may seem obvious, its origin is not. Like many of the world's deserts, the American deserts lie in a belt above the Tropic of Cancer. The rest of the world's deserts lie in a belt below the Tropic of Capricorn.

The distribution of deserts stems from the earth's rotation. Air heated at the equator rises and moves across the tropics and toward the poles. As it is cooled and reheated and jostled in wind currents, it alternately picks up and drops moisture.

Warm, moist air brought by the prevailing westerlies approaches the West Coast from the sea and is chilled by cold water currents that flow from Alaska to the Pacific coast. The air then collides with the Sierra and Cascade mountains and is deflected upward. Further cooled by the altitude, the air drops its cargo of moisture on the western slopes. By the time the air descends the eastern slopes of the mountains, it is usually dry. That is why the American deserts exist.

Of course, low rainfall alone does not make a desert, or the Arctic would be included. To qualify as a desert, a land's evaporation rate must greatly exceed its precipitation. In the desert, the combination of low humidity, nearly constant winds, and hot, unclouded sunlight helps make the rate of evaporation very high.

The desert's limited cloud cover has a double-edged effect on the harsh climate. During the day, there is little chance for rainfall and little to deflect the sun's rays, giving the desert its high temperatures. And after sundown, when the desert's hot surface radiates heat upward, the clear skies let the heat quickly escape. This dearth of insulation makes the desert prone to great swings of temperature from day to night. The temperature may be a summery 75 degrees on a January day in Death Valley, for example, yet go below freezing at night, as if moving from season to season in hours instead of months.

Understandably, such conditions put fierce demands on desert plants and animals. Yet life abounds; for the desert, despite some outward appearances, is not a wasteland, but a place of clever, streamlined economy.

Whether or not this economy has the look of a wasteland is all in the eyes of the beholder. With their monotonous growth of low sagebrush and shadscale scrub, much of the northern deserts may seem the very characterization of desolation—largely treeless and spottily colored, the green gray of their low shrubs and the warm brown of their bare earth predominating. Yet, for their wildlife inhabitants, the Great Basin and Painted deserts represent not a wasteland but a refuge.

With mild summers and winters as cold as those on the prairie, the northern deserts contain alternate

The Great Basin Desert covers 200,000 square miles in a series of dry basins such as this salt flat backdropped by Nevada mountains. The monotonous vegetation belies this desert's abundant animal life. The adaptable, quick-witted coyote finds plenty to eat here.

habitats for their high-mountain dwellers and for the creatures that inhabit their hotter basins. In summer, the peaks offer relief from the heat in the basins; in winter, the basins offer relief from the cold of the mountains. In winter, for example, many mule deer move from the mountains to the desert floor where snowfall is much lighter and food for grazing is readily available.

The dominant vegetation in the northern deserts is sagebrush, which is so pervasive it has given the region its alternate name of Sagebrush Desert. The most widespread plant in the West, these bushy, gray green shrubs grow in clumps with open space between them. They cover nearly all terrain in the northern deserts except the salt flats, where the dull-gray shadscale scrub, a low bush, takes over. On mountains, sagebrush gives way to a desert woodland of low, crooked trees—piñon pine and juniper—and, if the mountain is high enough, to full coniferous forests and snow-covered peaks.

Sagebrush is not just food, but also home, shelter, and shade for many northern desert animals, some of whom carry their special affiliation with the plant in their names. The sage grouse, a large, drab bird colored in the gray green of its namesake, is totally dependent on sagebrush. It builds its nests beneath the plant and feeds on its leaves. The sage thrasher and sage sparrow, also a muted grayish brown color, build nests of sage bark in the sagebrush's branches and feed on its seeds. Below them, the small sagebrush lizard—gray brown on its back and blue on its belly—scampers on the open ground in search of insects and retreats to the branches of the shrub when threatened. And the gray sagebrush chipmunk emerges from its underground burrow to snatch insects and seeds from the plant.

Many of the creatures on the northern deserts are small rodents, and most of those are mice. One of the most interesting is the little grasshopper mouse, who seems to have adopted some of the habits of its enemy the coyote. With soft, light-tan fur and a short tail, the

mouse—perhaps staking out its territory—stands on its hind legs and gives a long, high-pitched howl. When eating, it holds its struggling prey—usually a grasshopper—in its forepaws and gulps down the ill-fated insect head first. This fierce mouse will also eat lizards—even other mice!

Another creature, not quite as common as the mice but usually more visible, is the desert cottontail. This rabbit is quiet during most of the day, flattening itself in a shady hollow in the soil to await sundown when it emerges—warily—to nibble on plants. When threatened, it huddles behind rocks or low shrubs or, if lucky, dives into another animal's nearby burrow.

The cottontail has good reason to be cautious. A coyote may be lurking somewhere nearby, and coyotes do their best to make rabbits a main part of their diet. Another enemy is the kit fox, a sandy-colored animal that has large, triangular ears and is about the size of a small dog. The fox digs its home in the desert soil and hunts after sundown, using its big ears to scoop up the secretive mewlings and rustlings of nocturnal prey.

One of the kit fox's prey is the spotted skunk, itself a predator of small rodents, insects, and snakes. To discourage its predators, this little skunk, about the size of a large kitten, adds an interesting twist to its relatives' famous and time-tested method of repelling enemies. When threatened, it does a handstand and waves its full, bushy tail overhead. Any attacker who doesn't heed this warning is sprayed with the skunk's powerful and foul-smelling scent, also an irritant to the eyes. The scent is not a guaranteed deterrent, however; if hungry enough, a predator can always choose to ignore it.

One thing no small desert animal can afford to ignore is the bright, cloudless sky. In the desert's wide, open spaces, small animals are easily visible to the large predatory birds that soar overhead. In a matter of seconds, a hawk, owl, falcon, or eagle can dive from the sky and scoop up prey—a mouse, lizard, or rabbit—and yank it into the air and out of sight.

Yet, ironically, it was the predatory skill of one of these great birds—the golden eagle—that once threatened it as a species. A large, graceful bird with probing, golden eyes and a wingspan of over six feet, the golden eagle was killed in great numbers prior to 1962 because it was thought to prey on the lambs and kids of domestic sheep and goats. But although some such losses do occur, they are relatively few. Rabbits form the bulk of the bird's diet; it also eats a diverse collection of other prey, including insects, turtles, and skunks. Golden eagles are now protected by law.

An especially somber-looking bird, the turkey vulture also snatches small animals from the ground. But in its cloak of dark feathers, it seems better dressed for its

The lives of sagebrush flat denizens are woven together in a rich web. A desert cottontail (right) feasts on the tough shrubs while a kit fox (above left) hopes to catch the rabbit off guard. A patrolling golden eagle (above) might make a meal of either one.

main duty as undertaker of the desert. Like its smaller relative, the black vulture, the turkey vulture dines primarily on carrion. Ugly by any standards except, perhaps, those of another vulture, the naked-headed bird has a beauty in flight that is rarely surpassed. It soars gracefully, even elegantly, on updrafts of warm air, only occasionally flapping its wings as it skims over the desert on the lookout for its next meal.

Viewed from the height of a soaring bird, the desert reveals spectacular canyons that easily pass unnoticed by viewers on the ground. Unchecked flash floods and persistent streams and rivers have wedged themselves deeper and deeper into the floors of the American deserts. Names like Devil's Washbowl, Bruneau

81

Canyon, Canyon de Chelly, and Grand Canyon denote but a scattering of these clefts with steep walls.

The greatest of these canyons, of course, is the Grand Canyon. It is the world's largest erosion fissure, a sight of breathtaking beauty. A monument to the awesome powers of erosion, it has been carved over a period of about ten million years by the Colorado River at the painstaking rate of less than an inch a century. Now 6,500 feet deep, it cuts across the Colorado Plateau in Arizona for 250 miles.

Because the Grand Canyon is so deep yet cuts through a high, uplifted plateau that escapes the grasp of the desert, it offers wildlife an exceptional variety of habitats. At one end of the scale are the cool, coniferous forests of the plateau. At the opposite end is the scorching desert of the canyon bottom. There, moisture left by the scant rainfalls is quickly evaporated and temperatures climb to 120 degrees in the summer, rivaling the worst the southern deserts have to offer.

Though the Grand Canyon is exceptional, it is not alone in its offerings to wildlife. Wherever canyon walls descend dizzyingly straight downward, birds may nest with little fear of predators, save of bigger birds.

One common bird of desert canyons, the cliff swallow, supplements its insect diet with the fruit of junipers it finds growing high on the rocky cliffs. While the towering cliffs offer little to challenge adult swallows, they can be deadly to flightless chicks or hapless eggs. The bird takes great care to construct a safe fortress. Each member of a mated pair gathers mouthfuls of mud which it plasters to the canyon walls, eventually building a bottle-shaped nest with a single small opening into its cradling interior.

Even the rare peregrine falcon, who does not construct its own stick nest, is mindful of the danger that cliffs present to its smooth, rounded eggs. It digs a small hollow in the soil on the cliff edge so that the eggs will not roll out. The falcon's diet consists largely of other birds—including the cliff swallow.

Steep, desert-canyon walls offer cliff-dwelling birds nesting sites inaccessible to most predators. In the Grand Canyon (left) the rare peregrine falcon (below) hollows out a nest in the soil on narrow ledges. Cliff swallows (right) build bottle-shaped cradles of mud on the walls.

Where cliffs are more gently terraced, canyons contain many secret places for larger wildlife. Desert bighorn sheep and mule deer find food and protection on slopes below canyon rims. And in some canyons, swirling waters have carved caves and crevices into the rock. Wind-blown sand has polished their walls, and water carrying fragments of oxidized metal has splashed them in warm and ruddy hues. Writing of such caves on his mid-nineteenth-century exploration of the Grand Canyon, John Wesley Powell likened them to a "marble pavement, all polished and fretted with strange devices, and embossed in a thousand fantastic patterns."

These smooth hideaways, sheltered from sun and wind, are perfect desert sanctuaries. A female cougar will seek them out for her cubs, who spend the early months of their lives there, until they are old enough to accompany her on hunting expeditions. A sculpted palace amidst rugged rock, their cave is a sheltered, cool spot in a brutally hot environment.

At the bottom of a south-
western canyon, a cougar
finds the right ingredients
for raising her cub: a
reliable source of water
and a ready-made den.

While fierce weather conditions in canyons may be tempered, they are unfettered elsewhere in the wide-open southern deserts. There, the benefits of mild winters are offset by the long, hot summer, when temperatures normally top 100 degrees. Because conditions in the southern deserts are so harsh, plants and animals that live there must be highly specialized and are united by an obsessive preoccupation: the procurement and preservation of water. For even in this dry land, water is still the main ingredient of life.

Most desert animals avoid water loss and overheating as best they can by avoiding the hottest part of the day. Consequently, in one way or another, at one time or another, most desert animals—rodents, horned lizards, and spadefoot toads, to name only a few—cover themselves. Lizards hide in burrows and cracks in rocks or under ledges; foxes and rodents also burrow to escape the scorching heat of day. Further, the latter tend to be nocturnal. They thereby not only avoid the hot sun, but also make it more difficult for predators to find them. Animals in the hot deserts also tend to be small. The problems of feeding and keeping a large body cool and moist are too great in this land of little rain. While the pronghorn may be said to typify prairie animals, the desert has a much smaller creature as its quintessential representative: the kangaroo rat.

Neither a rat nor a kangaroo, this tiny critter is a specialized mouse with powerful hind legs and furred "sand shoe" feet that enable it to jump almost two feet high. Tan furred, dark eyed, and long tailed, this solitary creature shares its burrow only with the dry seeds that make up its diet. Oddly, its underground storehouse may hold pounds and pounds of them, plenty enough to share. Yet it meets others of its species only to mate. Other encounters are likely to result in leaping scuffles.

This nocturnal creature is so careful to shun the heat associated with light that it will not even venture from its burrow during a full moon. But the trait that makes the kangaroo rat a master of the desert is its ability to live without drinking water. Its nocturnal habits prevent the loss of moisture to the sun, and its body manufactures all the moisture it needs from its diet of dry seeds.

Water-conserving adaptations such as these are shared by all desert life, including the plants. Their surprising bounty is a measure of their success. The most widespread plant in the southern deserts is the creosote bush, a three- to four-foot-tall shrub with shiny evergreen leaves. This remarkably drought-resistant plant

In deserts like the Sonoran of Arizona (right), escaping the blistering heat is basic to survival. A desert jackrabbit (left) sprawls in a precious patch of shade; a kangaroo rat (below) relies on the coolness of its burrow.

can survive in areas that go rainless for over a year. It cuts its water loss during drought by shedding leaves, twigs—even branches—but it retains small, immature leaves for better days.

Part of the plant's success seems more diabolical in nature: It is thought that its roots release into the soil toxins that prevent competing bushes from taking root. Thus there is open ground between plants. This wide spacing of plants is not limited to the creosote bush, however; it is widespread among desert vegetation—and with good reason. The less a plant shares its plot of land with others, the better its chances of obtaining water and of surviving.

Likewise, many other plants practice the creosote's habit of shedding leaves during drought, for the wind and sun can steal much water from their thin surfaces. The tall, whiplike ocotillo sprouts many small leaves in times of moisture, then quickly loses them during drought. The plant can do this up to eight times a year.

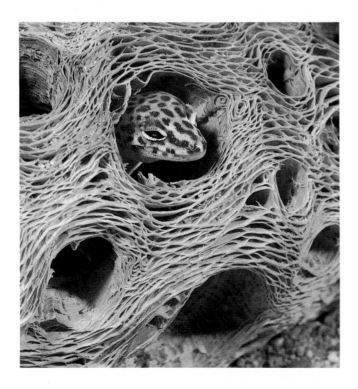

Hard, spiny desert plants offer cozy protection to some desert dwellers: A banded gecko (far left) finds cool shade in a cholla skeleton; a mourning dove (left) nests in a cavity in a saguaro; and a cactus wren (above) disregards a cholla's spines while she constructs a fortress for her young.

on its sturdy arms, feed on the nectar of its white blossoms, and nibble on its juicy red fruit.

Few saguaros reach their full height, for the plant's early life is a treacherous one. As a seedling, it is at the mercy of nibbling rodents, a condition it does not quickly outgrow. A ten-year-old saguaro is only four inches high. Not until the plant has survived sixty or more summers does it sprout the arms that give it the look of a supplicant in appeal to the heavens.

In recent years, the saguaro—and many other cacti—has become a hostage of sorts as cactus rustling has become more and more profitable. With the recent surge of population in the Southwest, the demand for cacti for use in decorative landscaping has increased. While most desert states have laws protecting their plants, the laws are difficult to enforce and the desert is continually being stripped of its hardy native plants.

Cacti were not always viewed so covetously, however. One early California missionary, having had his fill of the spiked plants, wrote, "Thorns are surprisingly numerous, and there are many of frightening aspect. It seems as if the curse of the Lord, laid upon the earth after the fall of Adam, fell especially hard on California and had its effect."

If the thorns of many cacti do not receive admiration, they do demand respect. Generally, they are quite effective at discouraging animals from nibbling at the juicy flesh of these plants. Some creatures, however, have a valuable talent for dodging the sharp spikes and thus are able to use the cactus to fullest advantage.

The chain cholla cactus—named for its "chains" of cylindrical, fiercely spiked joints—is notorious for its spikes sharp enough to pierce leather with just a touch. Chain cholla are also known as jumping cacti. Their joints are so easily dislodged that they seem to jump at the hiker who carelessly brushes the plant with his pant leg—where he'll find the segment firmly and painfully affixed. Yet the cactus wren, a brown-and-white speckled bird about the size of a robin, takes no apparent

Another group of desert plants has taken this method to a greater extreme by dispensing with leaves altogether. These are the cacti, classic landmarks of the southern deserts. Their thick, green trunks have taken over the important food-producing process of photosynthesis that is performed by the leaves of other plants. A cactus's thick, waxy coating also helps it preserve water by preventing evaporation.

With an incredible variety of shapes and sizes, the cactus offers desert wildlife a great array of shelter, shady spaces, food, and nesting sites. Even in death it is useful to wildlife, for its woody inner skeleton makes a fine home and hiding place for small desert creatures.

The tallest of the cacti, the saguaro, is often so full of wildlife it resembles an apartment building. This cactus, which can reach fifty feet in height and live up to two hundred years, is a favorite of desert birds. The tenant list includes elf owls, doves, hawks, vultures, and many more. Birds hollow out nesting holes in its trunk, perch

notice of the spikes as she darts onto the cactus with a load of plant fibers carried in her beak. The large, domed nest she is constructing on the cactus will be a secure haven for her young, for the cholla fortress makes her nest almost completely predator proof.

Another creature nearby is having a feast few others would dare attempt. The peccary, a sturdy animal with coarse fur and a blunt snout, roams the desert in small groups. When a peccary stops for a bite at a low prickly pear cactus, it doesn't let the spines deter it; it eats them.

Like most desert life, the prickly pear is a plant that down to the finest detail of its construction seems mindful of the sun's scorching rays . The plant grows in low clumps of flat, elliptical pads jointed in such a way that the narrow sides of the pads usually receive the full brunt of the midday sun, protecting the majority of the plant's surface from the harsh, drying light.

While many desert animals, such as the cactus mouse, are able to climb cacti in search of a meal, some, such as the peccary, cannot. For these creatures, the low-growing prickly pear is an important food source. One stoic desert standby, the desert tortoise, relies on the flowers and fruit of this cactus as part of its largely vegetarian fare. Its diet of cactus also provides some moisture, but a built-in reservoir that lies just beneath the tortoise's upper shell provides most of the vital fluid when puddles and other water sources have disappeared. Recently, however, the tortoise's survival seems to have become more closely linked with the goodwill of man than with the bounty of the desert.

The desert tortoise is a plodding creature with no real defenses save its shell—a little over a foot in length in adults—which protects its body and head from the sharp claws of prowling predators. Unfortunately, the shell offers no protection against wildlife collectors, for whom the large tortoise is a favorite and easy catch.

In the race for survival in the desert, the hare—not the tortoise—is coming out ahead. The jackrabbit is one of the most common of desert animals. One species, the

Prickly pear cacti provide a variety of services to desert denizens. A peccary (top left) and a desert tortoise (bottom left) eat the pads—spines and all. A cactus mouse (right) builds its nest in a shady part of the plant.

antelope jackrabbit, is a remarkable runner. Able to flee danger in bursts of speed reaching 40 miles per hour, it is outdistanced only by its namesake, the pronghorn antelope. Like the pronghorn, the hare also has white hairs on its rump which it erects as a warning signal to others of its kind when it is fleeing danger.

It is a peculiar irony that one of the dry desert's dangers is a very wet one: the flash flood. A sudden desert cloudburst does not necessarily offer the relief one would expect it to. Often, the water comes down with such sudden force and in such great quantities that the dry, sun-baked soil cannot possibly absorb it all as it falls. Vast amounts of runoff collect in washes, where it gushes forward with tremendous force.

These flash floods erupt seemingly out of nowhere and come so suddenly they may catch animals and humans unawares. "I have stood in the middle of a broad sandy wash with not a trickle of moisture to be seen anywhere," remembers Edward Abbey, author of *Desert Solitaire,* "sunlight pouring down on me and on the flies and ants and lizards, the sky above perfectly clear, listening to a queer vibration in the air and in the ground under my feet—like a freight train coming down the grade, very fast—and looked up to see a wall of water tumble around a bend and surge toward me."

The cloudburst, which may bring an entire year's rainfall, is usually over in minutes. But the flood may rampage over the land for hours, uprooting cacti, forcing critters to flee, and carrying bushes atop its surly brown froth. Then, just as quickly, it ends and the meager quantity of remaining water seeps into the sandy soil. The only visible reminder of the storm is a bare, brown strip of land showing the scars of rushing water.

Fortunately for the desert, that is not quite all that remains. Some water does manage to penetrate the desert's deeper layers of soil, which usually retain some moisture below six feet. In the desert, this scant amount of water is enough to work miracles.

Around a sandy rise, tucked away in the cool, purple

One of the desert's greatest dangers is, ironically, a wet one. A single cloudburst (left) may bring an entire year's ration of rain. Resulting flash floods (top) tear up plants and soil. In the end, no water remains above ground (above)—just the dry earth scarred by the violence of the raging water.

shadow of a mountain, the oasis is a lost prospector's dream. Tall fan palms, top-heavy with cool green fronds, create a lush spectacle that shocks the desert-accustomed eye. Recent tracks of mule deer, mountain lions, and coyotes pattern the moist soil, and birds flutter overhead, nipping at the palms' firm black fruits.

The tall fan palms, the only palm tree native to the United States, are living reminders of the time long past when America's deserts were subtropical forests. A stand of desert palms is always an indication that a water supply is nearby. Unlike other desert plants, the palm cannot survive without a steady source of water. Consequently, most American oases are found where the palms' long roots are fed by canyon streams or the steady seepage of underground water. Because this ideal setting is so limited in the desert, the oases themselves are limited. In the United States, they are scattered only in parts of southern California and in one small area nestled in a mountain canyon in western Arizona.

In the late winter and early spring, a more immediate and widespread desert magic emerges. The desert's groundwater, replenished by winter rain, feeds desert plants as they stir with life in the warm spring sun. Suddenly, the desert is no longer a study in drab greens and parched browns, but a land of exuberant color.

Cacti and other desert perennials dress for this festival of color by sprouting vividly hued blossoms. Delicate and bright, the blossoms are a striking contrast to the tough, scarred, green plants that produced them.

In a few select canyons, the desert holds unexpected treasures: fan palms thriving in oases, and canyon tree-frogs hiding within the rustling fronds.

A special relationship perpetuates two desert species: The yucca moth pollinates the yucca plant, and the plant feeds the moth's brood.

Like all desert flowers, cactus blossoms rely on the industriousness of insects to pollinate them, an important relationship upon which the success of future generations of desert plants hinges. Between two desert dwellers, the yucca plants and a small moth, the *Pronuba,* this relationship is exquisitely specialized.

The yuccas, a group of plants with long, sword-shaped leaves, are members of the lily family, although the family resemblance is minimal. One of the most bizarre in appearance is the Joshua tree. A familiar sentinel of the Mojave Desert, this tree was christened by Mormon settlers making their way to Utah. These travelers saw in the plant's firm stance and outstretched limbs the image of Joshua, guiding them towards a promised land. The plant is covered with stiff, pointed leaves which bristle outward in bunches at the ends of its branches and lie flattened against its long, thin trunk. Other species of yucca, more large shrubs than trees, have short trunks and central flowering stalks capped in white blossoms and surrounded by stiff fans of leaves.

The yucca's flowers are pollinated exclusively by the female *Pronuba* moth as she moves from flower to flower. Although she is doing the yucca a favor, it is with a purely personal purpose: She is laying eggs in the plant's ovaries. The eggs will develop into larvae, which feed on the plant's developing seeds. The larvae eat only a portion of the seeds, however, before they bore their way out and fall to the ground, leaving enough seeds behind to start many new yucca plants. The larvae then

burrow underground and emerge as adults one year later to carry on this mutually beneficial relationship.

The most spectacular of desert color appears not on the tall stems of a yucca or the gnarled forms of a cactus, but in the stretches of desert between them. Usually barren and brown, these spaces come to life briefly but brilliantly each year as seeds become seedlings, grow in a spurt, and blossom in their hasty rush to complete a full life cycle before drought reclaims the desert soil. So rapid is the appearance—and disappearance—of these flowering annuals that they are known as ephemerals.

For their brief seasonal lifespan—lasting days for some miniature flowers and only a few weeks at most for the others—the ephemerals deservingly steal the show from the desert's more stolid growth. For all their showiness, however, the ephemerals are equipped with a built-in sense of caution which makes their appearance unpredictable and all the more special. Unless nourished by the right combination of rainfall and temperature, a mix that varies from plant to plant and from one desert region to another, the plants will not blossom. They remain as dormant seeds locked in the soil until their conditions are met.

This inbred sense of caution even includes a means of separating a nourishing rainfall from a harmful one. Fewer ephemerals sprout following a torrential rain than following a gentle shower, even when the amount of rainfall is the same.

A few weeks later, the show has ended. The parent plants have died, and the desert floor reemerges, parched and sandy brown as ever. But the goal of the ephemerals—the single reason for their fast-paced existence—has been reached. Below the desert's surface, a hidden splendor lies. For a year, maybe more, countless seeds will remain dormant in the soil, awaiting the right combination of moisture and heat that will call them to the fore for their brief season in the sun. As ever, the desert's true beauty emerges not despite its fierceness, but because of it.

Land of Compromise:
THE WETLANDS

T here is something magical about a wetland. Thick with legend and folklore, it is a place, moreover, where fanciful tales seem plausible. But if the ghost of an Indian maiden paddling forlornly through the Great Dismal Swamp turns out to be nothing more than a wisp of swamp gas or a large white bird silently gliding over the water, the most remarkable aspect of the wetland will have survived intact.

As a whole, America's wetlands are its most productive wildlife habitats. Rich in food, water, and voluptuous plant growth, they are home to a teeming diversity of wild creatures.

Neither land nor water, but a melding of the two, wetlands hang in a state of tension and delicate balance. Too much water can drown them out of existence. Too little, and they vanish as well. Wetlands creatures reflect this tension: Adapted to water, most are, by necessity, still fully at home on land.

Aside from the great natural wealth of America's wetlands, there is one important reason why they are such bountiful wildlife habitats. It is a reason that is both a disadvantage and an advantage to the wetlands: Wetlands are areas for which most humans have little use. Since they have little obvious value to humans, many wetlands have been slated for "improvement" and drained at an alarming rate. America, in fact, now has only a little over half of its original wetlands. But this same human disdain has left some inaccessible wetlands or portions of wetlands relatively untouched. Here, in these near-pristine places, animals live in relative peace. So valuable are these precious few places for wildlife that some creatures threatened with extinction—the Everglade kite, the Mississippi sandhill crane, the Florida panther—manage to hold their own here. All wetlands, however, hold their treasures, though perhaps not so rare as these. One has but to enter a wetland to see a pageant of nature come to life and to glimpse wild America as it must have been in its earlier days.

A mother's redoubt: From her nest mound, a trumpeter swan fiercely defends the future of her brood in Yellowstone National Park.

The marsh "...is a place that seems often unable to make up its mind whether it will be earth or water, and so it compromises."

—Harnett T. Kane

Water lilies add a delicate touch to the aura of mystery in Georgia's Okefenokee Swamp. Water lilies are floating nurseries for beetles, snails, and damselflies.

100

In broad terms, America's wetlands fall into three basic categories: bogs, marshes, and swamps. A bog is a deep pool of stagnant water overlain with a mat of spongy, light-green sphagnum moss and fringed by coniferous trees. A marsh is a shallow, treeless wetland dominated by rushes, grasses, and sedges. And a swamp is a wetland that supports trees and shrubs.

But any rule applied to wetlands must be an extremely flexible one, for they are mutable places, and these divisions are not as clear cut as they may sound. For starters, the land/water equation constantly changes. Some areas are flooded for only part of the year. Others, such as those that form along the floodplains of rivers, experience varying levels of water at different times of the year. Besides, a single wetland may display traits of more than one category.

Because of these factors, America's wetlands are wildlife habitats of incredible diversity. They take almost every conceivable size and shape, from tiny roadside ditches bristling with cattails to the 13,000-square-mile sweep of America's largest wetland, the Florida Everglades. They create vastly different worlds for wildlife, from an icy Michigan bog to Florida's humid subtropical Great Cypress Swamp, heavy in moss and mystery. The East Coast and Gulf states are also thickly fringed in salty, tidal wetlands; but these salt marshes will be explored in the following chapter.

Wetlands are as widespread as they are diverse. Every

America's wetlands take many forms and refresh almost every corner of the land: In northern Michigan, a mat of sphagnum creeps toward the watery center of a cold, spruce-fringed bog (below). In California, a tule marsh bordered by willows (right) offers cool respite from a hot day.

state has some—even arid Arizona and New Mexico. Most of America's wetlands, however, are clustered in Florida, Louisiana, North and South Carolina, and Texas. Mississippi, Arkansas, and Georgia also have many, as do Minnesota, Wisconsin, and Michigan.

As its name implies, a wetland is the merging of two very different substances—water and land—into a single unit. Yet, it takes much more than these two ingredients to make a wetland. Indeed, perhaps more than any other wildlife habitat, wetlands are largely products of the plant and animal life they support. This life shapes them, gives them their special character, and—eventually—unites them in a similar destiny.

Many wetlands, for example, begin as lakes. Bit by bit, season by season, dead plants and animals sink and accumulate on the lake's floor, reducing the water's depth. Tiny decomposers gradually break down this sediment, reducing the oxygen in the water and favoring plants over the animals that might help clear plants away. Eventually, marshy plants that fringe the lake's edges begin to encroach farther inward. And occasional or seasonal droughts allow plants to gain a greater roothold by exposing more land.

Usually, this plant growth develops in distinctive stages. First, plants able to grow in water move into the open spaces of a bog or marsh. Then, as land becomes more dominant, shrubs may follow. Eventually, trees may grow there, transforming the bog or marsh into a swamp and, with further drying, into a forest. Every lake is, thus, a potential forest in the making; and every wetland, a transitional link between these two worlds.

This transition is not necessarily one easily witnessed, for it takes a long time and meets obstacles along the way. In the Everglades, for example, periodic drought and flooding have helped keep its future forest in check: Trees are less tolerant of such changeable conditions than grasses. Fire, too, holds back trees by sweeping over the Everglades' sawgrass plains during the dry season. Those trees that do exist among the sawgrass are mostly fire-tolerant pines and palms. They grow on rounded green mounds, called hammocks, that poke through the sea of grass much as islands dot an ocean.

Wetland animals, in likewise well-devised acts of destruction, create conditions that help maintain their special habitat. In the Everglades, the alligator helps keep the creeks that lace the land free of clogging sawgrass roots by ripping at them with its teeth, thereby preventing the plants from spreading. Elsewhere in the country, the beaver creates new wetlands as it dams up streams. Its smaller relative, the muskrat, helps keep marshes free of dense, clogging plant growth by eating great quantities of marsh reeds, grasses, and cattails. Muskrats and carp also help deepen the marshes by uprooting water plants, which carry chunks of sediment with them as they float to the surface.

Of all wetland types, the bog is the one most com-

A sunlit northern swamp in Washington State (below) contrasts with a southern cypress swamp studded with flowering epiphytes (right). No matter what their differences are, swamps are one of America's most productive wildlife habitats.

pletely a world unto itself, for it has a unique grouping of plants to carry out its lake-to-forest transformation. These plants must be highly specialized, for bogs are the harshest of wetland environments.

Bogs occur almost exclusively in formerly glaciated regions of the country. As the glaciers receded, they left huge chunks of ice imbedded in the earth. When these chunks melted, they formed deep lakes within their impermeable rock cradles. Known as kettle hole lakes, they have become the bogs of today.

The most characteristic plant in the bog is the spongy, light-green sphagnum moss. Feathery and highly water absorbent, it floats on tiny gas-filled balloons. Its wind-borne spores germinate in water, slowly spreading the sphagnum mat. The water willow, another bog plant, sends floating branches across the surface of the bog, leapfrogging its way to the center, or watery eye. This combination forms a dense, buoyant mat of plant growth that encircles the bog and continuously creeps closer and closer to its watery brown center.

The tea color of the water comes from the thick layer of slowly decomposing peat that forms under the sphagnum mat. Formed of partially decomposed sphagnum and other plants, peat makes bog water highly acidic. Bog water also has little or no oxygen in it, making it a doubly trying environment.

While creating a harsh habitat in the water, these combined traits have invoked evolutionary responses in a special group of plants that seem straight out of a science fiction movie. These fascinating bog natives are the insectivorous, or insect-eating, plants.

Because the water has little oxygen, plant material in the peat decomposes very slowly, keeping valuable nutrients locked in the dead plants rather than releasing them into the water where other plants can use them. This is where a diet of insects comes in handy. Insectivorous plants eat insects to obtain the nutrients—nitrogen, phosphorous, potassium, and others—they cannot glean from the food-stingy water.

The nutrient-poor bog (left) fosters many insect-eating plants: Sundews (below) trap food on sticky drops; Venus flytraps (bottom) snap them between their leaves; pitcher plants (bottom right) drown insects inside their leaves. A red-spotted newt (top right), one of the bog's few animal residents, rests on a carpet of hair cap moss.

The best-known of these plants is the Venus flytrap, which snaps insects between its clamshell-shaped leaves. Several other insectivorous plants inhabit the bog, however, and each species has its own diabolically clever way of entrapping its prey. The vibrant sundew has small leaves covered with thick, straight hairs. At the end of each hair suspends a glistening drop of very sticky fluid. An insect that touches the liquid is held in place as the leaf closes around it and digests it.

In the final stages of a bog's life cycle, the mat of sphagnum and other plants completely covers the water, and trees begin to grow on it (right). Gray jays (above) and other birds now become permanent residents, and moose (far right) cross the cushiony mat on their way to the nearby forest.

Another insectivorous plant, the pitcher plant, has a sculpted beauty to it. Its large, vein-etched leaves look and function like pitchers, with a pool of water forming inside each one. The inside wall of the leaf is smooth and lined with hairs pointing downward, all the better to block any attempts to escape: Unlucky insects drown.

The plant is, in fact, such a good insect trap that some opportunistic insects have developed ways of exploiting its success to their advantage. Some flies will enter the pitcher when its water level is low and feed on the partially-digested bodies of the insects at its base. An ingenious female wasp takes more decisive action by chewing a hole in the side of the pitcher so that its water drains out. She then converts it into a nursery. She makes a grass nest inside the leaf, stocks it with stunned caterpillars, and lays an egg there. A species of mosquito goes one better. It, too, lays its eggs inside the leaves. There, the larvae develop unharmed by the trap and

with a ready-made supply of the rich nutrients the plant was saving for itself.

The very traits that give the bog its fascinating plant life have limited its animal life. Indeed, if a bog were the only wetland one visited, one might think of wetlands' reputation as renowned wildlife habitats to be gross exaggeration. The bog has none of the abundant aquatic life associated with other wetlands—no fish, no worms, no snails—for its water is too harsh. Likewise, few mammals live here permanently. Some may visit, such as moose which come to dip their snouts in the bog's murky water to graze. Occasionally, beaver and muskrat build their homes here. One of the few full-time mammal residents is the bog lemming. This rotund little rodent tunnels in the sphagnum and munches on grass. Perhaps the bog lemming, like the bogs themselves, is a remnant of the days of the glaciers. As the glaciers melted, the lemming may have been cut off from its relatives, the brown lemmings of Alaska and Canada.

The many layers of trees surrounding the bog make it a fine home for birds. Many northern species, including the yellow-bellied flycatcher, winter wren, swamp sparrow, gray jay, several warblers, and the golden-crowned kinglet, may be seen darting among the branches or heard brightening the day with their song.

Trees surround the bog in an orderly progression of species. In the dry land beyond the bog stand large trees like those in the surrounding forests. Closer in, where the water keeps the area cool and moist, coniferous trees such as black spruce predominate. Nearer still, the smaller, light-loving larch and low evergreen shrubs such as the leatherleaf venture out into the sphagnum mat. Sedges and the sphagnum itself take over near the bog's watery center and, given time, engulf it.

Even when the bog has been completely covered by the feathery green mat, the water beneath still asserts itself. With each footstep of large animals crossing it, the entire mat quakes, sending trees many yards away shivering with its undulating motion. It will take many,

many seasons before the encroaching forest makes the bog totally forgotten.

In contrast with the quiet, closed-in mystery of the bog, the freshwater marsh emerges as a wide-open world bursting with life. Like other wetlands, the marsh begins as a larger, deeper body of water. But unlike the bog, the marsh is a habitat not for a specialized few, but for a boisterous many.

As a pond ages, decaying plants and animals accumulate in ever-greater quantities on its muddy floor. Plants—cattails, bulrushes, pondweeds, and grasses—take root along the pond's edges. As the pond continues its transition into a marsh, the plants move farther toward the center of the pond. Unlike the floating sphagnum mat in the bog, most marsh plants take root in the rich, nutritious mud. Where the water is deeper, water lilies emerge. With increasing amounts of vegetation, water flow slows and the buildup of decayed plant matter that nourishes other plants increases, hastening the development of the marsh. Increased humus encourages the widespread growth of floating plants such as duckweed, which do not root in soil but take their nutrients directly from the water—a marsh is born.

But what makes the marsh such a distinctive habitat are its distinctive residents, which are attracted to the wetland in great number by the food and cover offered by its lush vegetation. The most noticeable marsh residents are the migrating birds, which arrive in huge flocks to nest or rest during their long journeys. But the marsh is home to many more creatures—permanent residents and visitors—most of whom, like the marsh itself, have lives defined by water. Muskrats, ducks, geese, and most of the other permanent residents of the marsh even have bodies shaped by their watery habitat: webbed feet, special insulation to ward off the water's chill, and fur or feathers tolerant of water.

The most powerful way in which the marsh's water may affect its wildlife residents, however, is by disappearing. Drought and changing water levels are com-

A marsh is the meeting place for a boisterous many: On stopovers on their arduous voyages, hordes of migratory waterfowl replenish their energies from the marsh's generous food supply.

mon phenomena in marshes and constantly shape the form and direction of its plant growth. The most successful marsh animals, needless to say, are those that can adapt to an ever-changing environment.

In the early morning hours, when a warbler's lyrical call sails through air still heavy with mist, the marsh stirs to life. In each of the marsh's zones—the grassy banks, the shallow water, and the open, deeper water at its center—creatures begin their day's activities. Around the edges of the marsh, where temporary visitors are most likely to congregate, a raccoon is already hard at work. It dips its slender black hands in the water and pulls them out holding a crayfish.

Across the marsh, tall reeds rustle softly and two white-tailed deer tentatively emerge to explore the water's edge. Looking for all the world like two cautious school girls at their first dance, they hesitate, briefly taking in the scene with their large, dark eyes. Then they step forward and drink from the marsh's water. The marsh's long reeds form a protective green curtain that hides them as they quench their thirst.

Beneath the deers' delicate hooves, other tracks pattern the mud. A mink has already visited the marsh this morning. This sleek, fierce predator even of marsh mammals as large as the muskrat has had smaller prey in sight today. Its tracks suggest it aimed to make a meal of one of the marsh's many frogs.

The moist marsh is a haven for reptiles and amphibians. Disturbed by the deer, the frogs react swiftly,

A day in the marsh bustles with activity: White-tailed fawns (far left) cautiously approach to quench their thirst; a pickerel frog (left) lands on a lily pad; a marsh rabbit (bottom right) hides in the reeds on the bank; and a purple gallinule (top right) steps on lily pads as it ventures across the water.

plop-plop-plop-plop-plopping into the water. Nearby, a painted turtle suns itself on a rock and a snapping turtle languidly lowers its head into the water. From a stand of dewy grasses, a glistening salamander emerges, and with a swift and silent move a water moccasin lunges to claim it. The poisonous snake then vanishes into the reeds without a trace.

Now swimming in deeper water, the snapping turtle leaves behind it a widening wake that teases the sunlight into ribbons and sparkles. Elsewhere, a marsh rabbit, another powerful swimmer, with its fur matted down and its rounded ears flattened against its neck, efficiently churns through the water. The marsh rabbit constructs a nest on the grassy bank of the marsh. There the rabbit will find shelter within the low plants, which it will also nibble on, roots and all, for dinner. When threatened, it makes a mad dash for the water, where it may outswim some enemies and outwit others by floating as motionless as a log.

Like the rabbit, many birds nest on the ground surrounding the marsh, where thick vegetation helps conceal their helpless brood from predators. Among these birds are the familiar mallard, the short-eared owl, killdeer, common woodcock, yellow-throated warbler, and king rail. One such ground nester is also a strong marsh predator. The harrier, or marsh hawk, flies low over the marsh, plummeting into the grasses and reeds after its prey—mainly mice, frogs, small snakes, even crayfish. Its keen sense of hearing, especially well-developed for a hawk, allows it to locate its targets among the marsh's many hiding places.

One of the most striking of marsh birds is the purple gallinule, a richly-colored water bird. Its main habitat is the sturdy reeds that fringe the water, where the bird builds a shallow basket of a nest suspended above the water. But the bird's long, widespread toes help expand its habitat to an area where few creatures its size would dare tread: the floating leaves of the water lilies. The gallinule's specially long feet help spread its weight

113

evenly, allowing it to take long, graceful strides across what otherwise would be very precarious footing.

The thick reeds that are home to the gallinule shelter many other creatures. Because the vegetation around the marsh grows in different heights and extends well into the watery center, it offers some protection from land-based predators. In addition to the gallinule, the swamp sparrow, common rail, long- and short-billed marsh wrens, and the red-winged blackbird nest there. Red-winged blackbirds are a boisterous influence around the marsh in spring, when the birds stake out nesting sites and bravely defend them from all kinds of invading foe. Not all red-winged blackbirds are easily spotted, though, for only half the species lives up to its name. The female lacks the glossy black feathers and brilliant red shoulder patches that characterize her mate; she is cloaked in earthen colors that help keep her invisible in her brown and tan cattail home.

As with many wildlife communities, however, the benefits a habitat offers are not without their accompanying drawbacks. While birds may nest in relative safety in the marsh cattails, sedges, and reeds, they face a problem of another sort: In this slippery, strictly vertical world, where is a bird to perch?

The solution of some marsh birds appears more an athletic feat than a comfortable resting posture: One leg firmly grips one reed, while the other is anchored on a neighboring reed. The solution works well unless the wind begins blowing or the bird is too small to reach from reed to reed. Then, the bird is left to improvise new solutions as best it can.

This hardy marsh vegetation is home to several other important creatures as well, although in these special cases the plants serve as building material rather than as ready made homes. The nutria and muskrat use the vegetation in great quantities, both as food and as construction material for the large, dome-shaped lodges they build in the middle of the marsh.

The nutria has an other-world look to it, perhaps deservedly so: This large rodent with a chunky body, large wedge-shaped head, and thick fur was imported from South America in 1899. Released in southern marshes, where it was hoped to breed and produce an ample crop of its luxuriant fur, it soon expanded its new-found range. It has now spread to southern Canada and coast to coast in the United States.

Even more widespread and more influential in the marsh is the muskrat. In its feeding and the building of its lodge, this large rodent has the capacity to reshape whole tracts of land. Weighing about three pounds, the muskrat looks very much like an overgrown mouse or vole. It has a full, rounded body, small eyes and ears, and a long, scaly tail. Awkward on land, it is swift and graceful in the water, where it may often be seen busily puttering about its lodge.

The muskrat first builds a base for its home, piling up reeds, sticks, and cattails harvested from the marsh's fringe and then plastering them together with marsh

A centerpiece of marsh life, a muskrat's lodge provides a home for many opportunists: Minks and raccoons make homes in abandoned ones; swans and ducks build nests atop them; even plants take root on the dry dome.

The tangle of cattails and bulrushes on its fringe surrounds a marsh with sound and motion. In its nest in the reeds, a female redwinged blackbird feeds her young (left). On the sidelines, a long-billed marsh wren (above) belts out its song from a cattail perch.

115

Draped in a green veil of duckweed, a muskrat (far left) emerges from the water after feeding on roots. A floating plant which gets its nourishment directly from the water, duckweed (below) covers much of the marsh's open water. Mallards (left) love to dine on duckweed.

mud. The floor of its domed home is constructed above water level, but contains convenient underwater exits. Outwardly a messy pile of vegetation, the lodge is actually a carefully blueprinted house that contains air vents in the roof and individual, grass-lined rooms.

Occasionally, when muskrat populations are large or abundant new growth in an emerging marsh entices them, they may eat out large patches of vegetation. If the grazed area is subsequently flooded, the plants die and the marsh's watery domain expands. While the "eat out" may cause considerable flooding, all this is well and good with the muskrat, for whom the watery center of the marsh is essential as a home.

Although dominated by water, the center of the marsh, like its other zones, is an active place with a vast array of niches for its wild residents to fill.

Understandably, many of these residents—both plants and animals—inhabit the area by floating. Small duckweeds, which grow unrooted in open water, form a carpet of light-green vegetation that can completely cover the surface of the water. As their name implies, these tiny plants are a favorite of ducks, which scoop them up with their bills in great quantities. But they also supplement the diet of larger animals such as muskrats.

Even the huge moose eats them as well as the delicate water lilies floating among them.

As is true in many wildlife habitats, what is food for some is home for others. The water lily, for one, functions as a microhabitat for a diverse range of tiny marsh creatures. Small frogs and insects live on top of its leaves; leeches and snails cling to its underwater stems.

The muskrat lodge is a similar microhabitat which, by no intent of its builder, houses opportunistic squatters as well as the original owner. Minks, mice, and raccoons may take refuge inside an abandoned one; ducks and terns nest on it; snails, leeches and small fish hide amidst its underwater branches; and terrestrial plants take root on its dry dome.

If the marsh's water level falls significantly, the muskrat lodge may serve an even larger function as it helps usher in a whole new world. On the muskrat lodge and all through the now-shallow marsh, plants gain greater roothold. Cattails, bulrushes, and sedges grow everywhere on the wet mud. In time, and if trees and shrubs move in, the marsh may become a swamp.

The word *swamp* has the power to evoke a potent visual image. The swamp of the mind's eye has dense plant growth; dark, foul water; humid, heavy, unmov-

In a subtropical cypress swamp in Florida, a great blue heron scans its domain from a cypress-knee perch. The knees may help the cypress trees breathe; they certainly provide the heron with an overlook from which to search for a meal.

ing air; an ever-present sense of danger. Who knows what strange creatures inhabit this mysterious place?

This concept of the swamp as a place of foreboding is typified in the name of one of America's largest swamps, the Great Dismal, which spans the Virginia-North Carolina border. Colonel William Byrd II, who explored the swamp in 1728, felt "Dismal" was a fitting appelation. He had a rather dour view of the place, which he termed a "horrible desert," where "the foul damps ascend without ceasing, corrupt the air and render it unfit for respiration....Never was Rum, that cordial of Life, found more necessary than in this Dirty Place."

For all the mystery and misconception that surrounds it, however, a swamp is, quite simply, a wetland with trees. But not any flooded forest may become a swamp. Only trees adapted to growing in standing water will survive; the others, like any other living thing unprepared to cope with flooding, will drown. Common swamp trees include the silver maple, red maple, American elm, Atlantic white cedar, Eastern cottonwood, black willow, and river birch. But the most spectacular of swamp trees and the one most evocative of the swamp's mysterious aura is probably the bald cypress. This sturdy giant of the temperate and subtropical swamps may live to be 600 years old and serves as a centerpiece for the swamp's seething life.

The bald cypress is a deciduous conifer—that is, an evergreen that is not always green; it loses its needles in winter. The tree copes with its watery environment by sending up conical projections, called knees, that jut out of the water all around the cypress's trunk. Although their exact function is unknown, these knees probably help the plant obtain oxygen from the air. While old cypresses may stand in water several feet deep, young cypresses that have not developed knees will not grow in constantly flooded ground. They still rely on the oxygen their roots obtain from the soil.

While the swamp is a habitat with a wealth of folklore and a host of mythical inhabitants, its real riches are its

Trees in the swamp are vital avenues for many mammals living there. An endangered southern fox squirrel (right) scurries along a woody route. A raccoon (below) has come down a massive cypress tree to fish at its base.

wildlife residents. With its ample water supply and dense plant growth, the swamp provides the resources to support a myriad of creatures. As in any habitat, this web of life thickens and grows when these factors are combined with a warm climate, making subtropical swamps the richest, most populated homes of all.

Here, common critters share their home with some of the rarest. The Florida panther, with only 26 known animals in mid-1984, inhabits the Everglades and adjacent Big Cypress Swamp in Florida. The ivory-billed woodpecker, if it exists still, hangs on in swamps in the Big Thicket of eastern Texas. These creatures share their homes with familiar wild faces: raccoons, opossums, skunks, cottontails, hawks, warblers, and wrens. The special blessings and demands of the swamp unite this diverse group—and, at troubled times, may even make them forget their differences.

Author Bill Thomas, a long-time swamp observer, once watched as two swamp enemies, a bobcat and a swamp rabbit, together rode the current of the Mississippi River on a floating treetop as the flood swept through Louisiana's Atchafalaya Swamp. Although the large swamp rabbit—at nearly two feet long, America's largest—is a favorite prey of swamp-roving bobcats, neither paid much attention to the other, so absorbed were they in their predicament.

While large floods are an occasional factor in the swamp, standing water is a constant one. And with water, water everywhere, the lives of most of the swamp's birds and mammals center around the trees. The broad trunk of the cypress and its nubby knees offer excellent spots for a swamp animal to go fishing. Midway up a tree a fox squirrel, cloaked in a coat of warm russet, keenly watches the water. If frightened, the squirrel will quickly turn and scamper up the trunk to the shelter of its nest of leaves and twigs. Farther down, a raccoon probes the dark water for a crayfish or minnow.

The raccoon is not alone in his love for tasty crayfish. A snowy egret, slicing through the shallow water on its

sticklike legs, searches for a morsel. And many other wading birds, including herons and ibises, also probe the water for its rich aquatic life. Indeed, with so many fish-eating birds attracted to the swamp, a shortage of nesting space would seem to present a greater problem than a shortage of food. This is not the case, however. Although the quantity and variety of birds might lead to bickering over nesting sites, the birds exhibit a remarkable degree of cooperation. One study of a highly-populated, three-acre nesting colony in a swamp in Reelfoot Lake in western Tennessee, for example, found that the largely nocturnal black-crowned night heron tended to nest in the shady, lower tier of branches about 60 to 70 feet above ground; that the graceful, white, great egret tended to nest in the 80- to 90-foot range; and that the streamlined double-crested cormorant tended to make its home in the sunny, uppermost branches over 100 feet above ground.

The nesting level allocated to the cormorant appears

High in the trees, bird life predominates. A red-tailed hawk in the canopy (above) dries its wings after a light rain, and a cattle egret (right) tends its nest in the network of branches.

to work against its feeding strategy. For although the bird fishes by diving and even swimming for short distances under water, its home is high on the trees. But the cormorant's feathers are not well waterproofed, so the bird needs a sunny spot in which to dry them off.

With trees forming such a dense canopy overhead, plants seeking sunlight in the swamp usually must grow as high as possible. One strange group of swamp plants are the epiphytes, or air plants, which grow on the trunks of trees. These plants are not parasites, however; they take their nourishment directly from the atmosphere and rely on the trees only for support and as a way to reach the sunlight.

Many of these epiphytes, from a family called the bromeliads, are stiff-leaved plants that resemble the spiky shock of leaves atop pineapples. One epiphyte, Spanish moss, festoons swamp trees in great, feathery, gray green swatches. And the sinister-looking strangler fig begins life as an epiphyte when one of its tiny seeds is

dropped onto a tree by a bird. The fig's roots work their way earthward, wrapping their host in a deadly clinch. Overhead, the fig's branches grow to overshadow its host, cutting it off from sunlight. Eventually, the host dies, leaving the fig in its place.

Among the most dominant swamp animals is a creature that does not strain for the sunlight, but rules supreme from the muddy, murky floor of its home in southern swamps. This is the alligator. While hunters who trapped the huge reptile for its thick hide once endangered the species, it is now protected and finally is beginning to reassert itself. Although its eggs and young may become meals to other animals from time to time, the powerful adult alligator has no natural enemies. As a preeminent predator, however, it does not have a whole lot of friends, either.

A raccoon absorbed in fishing may not notice that the great, green log floating nearby has eyes—until the alligator lunges forward, grabs the unfortunate beast, and holds it under water until it drowns. A duck paddling on the surface of the water may, too, vanish as an alligator strikes from below and swallows the bird whole.

Although the raccoon and duck may not appreciate the reptile, the alligator, nonetheless, actually helps make the swamp a better home for its other wildlife residents. Like the muskrat in its marshy domain, the alligator acts to maintain its swamp home. By uprooting plants with its snout and tail, the alligator helps keep the swamp from becoming clogged with plants. It even benefits some of its cohabitants in times of drought by digging depressions known as gator holes.

With a gnashing and thrashing of snout and tail, the alligator deepens a hollow in the swamp floor. By working on it year after year, the gator may further deepen and extend the hollow until it assumes the dimensions of a small pond. During drought, gator holes may hold the only water in the swamp. These pockets of water dotting the dry expanse become responsible for saving the lives of countless small aquatic creatures as well as

Supreme ruler of the southern swamps, the alligator is this realm's most feared predator and its greatest benefactor. The alligator digs hollows, "gator holes," in the swamp's floor; in times of drought, these depressions are the only wet spots where birds like the green heron (above) can fish. Gator holes often hold the alligator's nest mound (left). From this guarded cradle comes a new generation of swamp overlords (above left).

123

Touched by the first light of dawn, Louisiana's Atchafa-laya Swamp stirs to life. As the sun parts the mists, the cries of herons pierce the air and the graceful flight of egrets ushers in the day.

the lives of the predators that rely on them for food. Alligators may even create water holes where there were none by digging through several feet of drying mud.

It is usually near one of these holes that the female alligator builds her nest, a great mound of grass, sticks, and mud generally about three to four feet high and six to eight feet long. As the nest may well be the highest spot of ground around, it serves as the hatching place not just for new alligators, but for many other kinds of life as well. Turtles may nest there; trees and shrubs take root there; other animals arrive to feed on and hide in the plant growth; and birds flock to nest in its branches. Given the right conditions, this mound of growth may become the starting point that transforms the swamp into another habitat, a dry forest. For like all wetlands, the swamp is another of nature's transitions—slow, graceful, and sure. Yet, enter a swamp in early morning and its future is easily forgotten as rising mists infuse it with the look of a primeval place that has always been there, and always will be.

To fully understand the value of wetlands, it is helpful to view them not merely as enchanted worlds, however, but as working parts of the environment. That wetlands are beneficial to the wildlife lucky enough to live in their midst is obvious. But wetlands also have a great deal to contribute to humans. Because their plants and spongy land are specially designed to absorb water, wetlands act as natural and efficient flood control systems. By holding water, they also help replenish the underground supplies that provide much of our drinking and irrigation water. Wetlands also act as natural water-treatment plants, helping to filter out pollutants, sediment, fertilizers—even heavy metals. Indeed, wetlands are so effective in this role that some small communities are experimenting with using wetlands instead of expensive treatment plants to purify partially treated sewage. A far greater value, however, and one more difficult to measure, is in what wetlands give to the lone human who stops there, watches, listens, and waits.

125

At the Edge of the Land:
THE COASTS

The scene is a timeless one: Waves flecked with foam swell and curve, becoming temporarily translucent in the sunlight. They arch, bend, and crash on the shore, buffeting the land with the inescapable dissension of two opposites forced to meet.

But while the action of the waves may be timeless, their effect on the edge of the land is immediate. America's coasts are wildlife worlds where not water, not land, but motion is the predominant characteristic. It is this endless motion that carves the land, creating straight, sandy beaches out of imposing cliffs, causing rock to fall and crumble.

This motion, too, colors the lives of the coast's wildlife residents and seems to have granted most of them fluid motion of their own. Shore birds take to the air above the sparkling water in patterns that twist and curve like the waves rushing ashore. The creatures of the sea have an allied grace as they maneuver its depths in shimmering, darting rivulets, or as they hold their own against the currents. And those creatures that, like the coast itself, are a product both of the sea and the land—the seals and sea lions—playfully bridge land, sea, and air in the arching curve of a single dive off rock and into the foaming surf.

Land and sea are not equal partners in the coast; in a test of power, the sea will usually prevail. But the land is not without its defenses. Tough plants growing in seaside marshes and swamps take firm hold of sediment with their twisting roots and fight back at the ocean by building more land. Grains of sand, as if endowed with some ancestral memory of the time when they were part of a cliff, form offshore barriers that protect the inner coast from the ocean's force. And the land itself, through its great rivers, deposits huge quantities of sediment in the path of the onrushing ocean, challenging the sea by creating new shores.

On Año Nuevo Island, off the coast of California, a sea-lion harem basks in the sun. Sea lions are perfectly adapted to life in the water, but, like all seals, must come ashore to breed.

"The shore is an ancient world, for as long as there has been an earth and sea there has been this place of the meeting of land and water. Yet it is a world that keeps alive the sense of continuing creation and of the relentless drive of life."

—Rachel Carson

The Pacific Ocean lashes at the Oregon coastline with thunderous waves. For those coast-dwelling animals which are able to cope with the sea's fury, the ocean provides a well-stocked pantry.

The ceaseless waves carve the land with varied artistry. On Bandon Beach in Oregon (left) crumbled remnants of mainland cliffs rest in the sea. At Año Nuevo in California (below), the sea has sliced terraces where tide pools form and where crabs feed during low tide.

America's most restless and most changeable habitat also has the dubious distinction of being its narrowest. Vast as the sea and the land are, the place where they meet is but nature's version of a line on a map. But America's coasts, seen through the eyes of the animals who bridge land and sea to live there, present qualities more important than those that may be measured with a yardstick. To these creatures, the coasts are a collection of wildlife worlds as diverse as any found on sea or land.

And what worlds they are! Steep, bare cliffs where the sea hurls itself with explosive force. Sweeping, sandy beaches beautiful as two deft strokes of an artist's brush—tan here for the sand, blue there for the sea. Quiet tidal marshes where the sea is lulled by thick reeds that sway gracefully in the current. And dense mangrove swamps of exotic beauty—and amazing durability. The characteristics of the coastlines that fringe the United States result from both the geologic history of the land and the ongoing struggle between the sea and the land.

The jagged, rocky New England shore is a classic example of what is called a drowned coast. Long ago, this hilly land was pushed down by the great weight of the glaciers it supported during the Ice Age. Then, as the glaciers melted, the immense quantity of water entering the seas raised the water level some 300 feet and flooded the world's coasts. In Maine, for example, former river valleys became estuaries, where osprey now harvest flounder, herring, and many other fish. And former

On most of the Atlantic Coast, the ocean has ground the land into sand and created long beaches. On a sandy beach in Florida, gulls harvest the food lapped ashore by the waves.

hilltops became islands where birds such as puffins and sea gulls now make their homes.

Although robbed of their former position by the glaciers, these hard, granite hilltops have proved to be a stiff opponent that has stood firm against the sea, eroding little. Not too far south, however, where the shore was made of softer material, the coastline has been continuously subject to dramatic changes caused by the sea itself. Cape Cod, Massachusetts, for example, is also a drowned coast. But because its cliffs are made of glacial deposits of sand and clay, the sea has been much more successful in carving the land.

When Henry David Thoreau looked out to the sea from the beaches of Cape Cod in the mid-Nineteeth Century, he found the relentless waves "too far-traveled and untamable to be familiar." Were Thoreau able to look at Cape Cod today, it would be the land that would not look familiar. For after 130 years of the sea's "nibbling at the cliffy shore where gulls wheel amid the

spray," as he wrote in *Cape Cod,* over two square miles of the narrow peninsula have been lost to the ocean.

While the rest of the Atlantic coastline was also flooded by the water from the melting glaciers, the way in which this coast meets the ocean has given it a much different appearance. South of New England, the land slopes gently to the sea from the mountains far inland. From Cape Cod to Florida and around to the shore of the Gulf of Mexico, the sea has created long stretches of sandy beaches. Because the ocean constantly shifts immense quantities of sand, these beaches are always changing, resulting even daily in a new sandy outcrop, a newly carved bend in the beach.

The load of sand carried by the waves and the currents might catch on a curve of the shore, eventually forming a sand spit. Given the right conditions, and enough sand, a sand spit will grow into an offshore barrier—among the largest and most influential creations at the ocean's edge. Where once there was open

The world of mangrove swamps emerges on the southern tip of Florida and on the Keys. Seedlings grow in salt water, extending the trees' domain into the sea.

water, whimbrels, sandpipers, and other shore birds will come to search for tiny worms and sand fleas.

Offshore barriers are a common feature all along the Atlantic Coast. They run parallel to the mainland and may eventually become full-fledged beaches in their own right. The beaches at Atlantic City, New Jersey, and Cape Hatteras, North Carolina, were formed this way. Because these barriers shield the shore from the full force of most of the ocean's waves, they help create new shorelines, give some protection to the old ones, and in some cases encourage the development of peaceful lagoons and saltwater marshes where wildlife can securely congregate.

Other spectacular features along the Atlantic Coast are those places where mighty rivers meet the sea. The Chesapeake Bay, for example, is a former complex river system, drowned when the ocean's level was raised. Today, its 4,600 miles of ragged shoreline, sending tendrils of water into Maryland and Virginia, cradle the richest marine estuary in the world. And in the Gulf of Mexico, where rivers have dumped their loads of sediment at the edge of the land, huge bulges have developed on the coast. The largest of these, the Mississippi Delta, is constantly being shaped by the Mississippi River, which daily delivers more than a million tons of sediment to the sea. Its delta has grown into an enormous mound of land whose exposed top extends for over 100 miles into the Gulf and whose underwater base extends much farther.

In contrast with the Atlantic Coast, America's Pacific shoreline is a place literally more straightforward in its approach to the sea. Here, the transition from land to sea is sternly abrupt—as if seeking a confrontation. And a confrontation is exactly what it gets. The waves that crash onto the Pacific Coast are larger and far more forceful than those on the Atlantic side. Prevailing west-to-east winds help fuel the Pacific Coast waves into impressive walls of water and foam.

America's western coastline is also much straighter than its eastern one. Inlets are few; the two most notable ones are Puget Sound in Washington and California's San Francisco Bay. And while a thin strip of pebbles or sand may lie at the base of the rocky cliffs, beaches are few and generally small. The dominant scenery is the stubborn rocks, resilient evergreen trees, and, of course, the ceaselessly crashing waves.

Unlike the Atlantic Coast, which was formed by a variety of forces, the Pacific Coast is largely a product of wave erosion. The pounding surf is a tireless sculptor, continuously carving the rock. In some places, waves have cut wide terraces that are covered with sea grasses. In others, great chunks of cliff were severed and now rest in the ocean in turreted formations called sea stacks. These formations and other broken pieces of land become resting places for seals and sea lions and perches for thousands of auklets, puffins, and murres.

This pounding habitat certainly seems inhospitable to the fragile fabric of life. "What right has the sea to bear in its bosom such tender things as sea-jellies and mosses, when it has such a boisterous shore, that the stoutest fabrics are wrecked against it?" Thoreau wondered. Yet, America's rocky shores, both on the East and West, are crowded with boisterous animal life.

The most numerous creatures are the sea birds, who nest in huge, squawking colonies on the rocky outcrops of the shore and on its islands. The roster of cliff-dwelling birds is awesome. Gulls, the ever-present bird of the shoreline, hoard islands all to themselves on both coasts. Stubby little auklets nest on the Pacific Coast. Puffins, whose somber black-and-white plumage is offset by the bright, clownlike coloring of their bills and feet, nest on two islands off Maine's coast and more widely along the Pacific Coast. Murres, the most abun-

Steep, rocky shores such as this one in Acadia, Maine (left), seem too sheer and harsh to invite any life. Yet seaside cliffs East and West teem with sea birds. Puffins (below), cormorants, and guillemots (right) find countless nooks and crannies to use as nests and perches and as lookout towers for spotting fish.

dant sea bird in the Northern Hemisphere, nest off Maine on America's Atlantic Coast and from Alaska to southern California on the Pacific. This bird is renowned for its huge nesting colonies. One at Three Arch Rocks, Oregon, is estimated to have some 750,000 birds.

This diversity of birds is supported, aside from a rich food supply, by the fact that the cliffs and islands offer a great variety of nesting sites. Auklets and puffins dig burrows in soil on the tops and on the sides of cliffs. Razorbills and murres nest on open ledges. And the black guillemot nests in crevices and between boulders near the sea.

All of these birds, however, are only the more visible part of a huge cycle of life that begins, of all places, on the floor of the polar seas. There, rich mineral nutrients give rise to an abundance of microscopic plant life. The minuscule plants get swept into two ice-cold currents that bathe America's East and West Coasts. The Labrador Current reaches down the northeast coast to Cape Cod,

which, by thrusting fifty miles out into the ocean, blocks the current's flow and separates the cool waters of the north from the warmer waters of the south. The California Current flows along the Pacific Coast from Alaska to California. In both currents, the rich microscopic plant life gives rise to larger microscopic animal life, both collectively known as plankton. Come spring, when these cold currents move nearer the surface, the plankton is at its peak. The flourishing plankton is food for millions of small fish which in turn are food for larger fish, ocean mammals such as seals and otters, and—of course—the many sea birds, providing ample nourishment for their huge nesting colonies.

The Labrador and California currents not only feed

the teeming life of ocean and shore, they also help give the shore its haunting atmosphere. The chilled water helps keep the surrounding air cool. Then, when warm air from the south blows over the cold water, a thick curtain of fog billows from the ocean. Flowing over the shores in dense mists, the fog nourishes the coniferous forests that grow on both coasts.

Although birds harvest a great deal of the wealth provided by the currents, they also help maintain this abundant food supply. Rain washes huge quantities of their excrement off the rocky cliffs and into the sea. There, it helps fertilize the water, contributing to the growth of plankton which may one day nourish the fish that will feed a future generation of ocean fliers.

The birds share the ocean's abundance of food—and the rocky shoreline—with another group of coast dwellers, the seals and sea lions. Descendants of land mammals—probably otters and bears—that returned to the sea some 25 million years ago, these air-breathing, warmblooded creatures are thoroughly adapted to life in the water. Still, they must return to the rocks for mating and the bearing of young.

The gray seal may be seen on islands off the coast of Maine and in Nantucket Sound, and the harbor seal, also known as the leopard seal for its spotted coat, may make occasional East Coast appearances. However, by and large, these creatures are a sight of the Pacific Coast. Other marine mammals that inhabit the Pacific Coast include the Northern, or Steller, sea lion; the Northern fur seal, famed for its soft, luxuriant undercoat; and the sleek, intelligent, and playful California sea lion, which cuts through the cold water like a brown torpedo.

Much of the life of the rocky coasts, however, is hidden by the waters of the restless sea and goes unseen by the land bound. Yet, even a confirmed land dweller may gain a glimpse of this life during low tide, when the waters move away from the rocks like a curtain parting at the beginning of a show to reveal myriad ocean worlds in miniature, the tide pools.

Rocky outcrops are ideal spots for marine mammals to haul out on. Harbor seals (far left) give birth to their pups there, and California sea lions (left) use them to take a break from their aquatic existence.

Tide pools are natural aquariums created when rocks trap sea water during the ocean's twice-daily retreat. But while these pools offer low-tide refuge to creatures that can't survive outside the water, they also become harsh environments that may push their inhabitants to the limits of survival. Because they are shallow, tide pools are subject to comparatively sudden changes. Rain may dangerously dilute the salt water. Conversely, the sun may evaporate the water, making the pools unbearably salty. The sun can also quickly heat them and rob them of the oxygen necessary for both plants and animals. As watery traps, they also make their denizens easy prey for birds and other predators.

Yet the fragile and quickly changeable environment in a tide pool is undeniably beautiful. Here, gentle currents created by the wind move the plants clinging to the rocks in a silent ballet. Fronds of brown, red, and green seaweed sway softly, covering and then uncovering the thick mosses and algae that grow on the rocks. Gradual-

Twice a day, when the sea retreats from the land, the rocky shore is left dotted with oceans in miniature. In the tide pools, starfish and anemones (left) await the sea's return; tiny crabs (below) scuttle across kelp strands; and gulls (far left) find a cache of food.

ly, other residents of the pool appear. Small fish and tiny, nearly transparent shrimp move from under their veil of weeds to dart across the crystal pool. A small crab scuttles over the pool floor, bypassing the purple, bristled forms of sea urchins that block its path.

Tide pools closest to the shore contain the largest and most varied assortment of ocean life. A small squid may dart under a rocky crevice as a sea cucumber ripples overhead, moving through the shallow water in slow but surprisingly graceful undulations. Among the loveliest of tide-pool creatures is the flowerlike anemone. Its beauty is a deadly one, however; with its blossom of stinging tentacles, it catches and digests small fish.

Like the anemone, much of tide-pool life survives the coming and going of the tides by clinging tenaciously to the rocks. Mussels cling like bunches of huge grapes, and ivory-white barnacles cement their shells in place, leaving the tiny animals inside free to sway with the current. The anemone, sea urchin, and starfish use the strong suction power of their many tube feet to anchor themselves in place. With this same power, the starfish pulls open the clamped shells of mussels and clams. If it can open the shell even as little as 1/25th of an inch, it has a meal. The starfish extends its stomach through its mouth and into the shell to digest its food. The small fish and crustaceans in the tide pool are also a ready source of food for gulls and other birds.

Though the sea otter also feeds on sea urchins, starfish, and other creatures found in tide pools, this accomplished fisherman is not one to take an easy meal. Rather than harvest its food from the pools, the large sea otter—adults are four to six feet long—may dive 100 feet or more to snatch its meals off the ocean floor.

Upon surfacing, an otter may immediately devour an especially challenging meal such as a pinching crab, but it usually takes its catch to its home in the kelp beds off the Pacific shore. There, it dines in leisure, floating on its back in its characteristic posture and using its belly as a

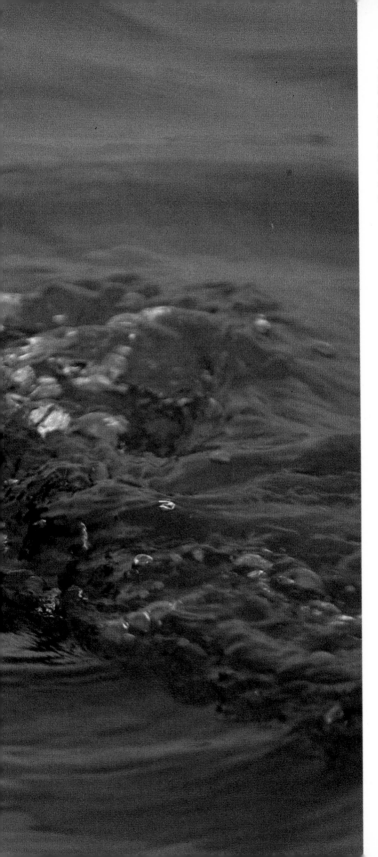

table. After eating, it indulges in a lengthy and elaborate grooming ritual. But the animal is not vain, merely practical; it relies on a layer of air trapped in its thick fur to help insulate it from the chilling water. If the fur becomes matted, it loses this insulating quality.

Although the sea otter's beautiful coat helps keep it warm, it has also been a liability. Men, seeking the otter's fur, overhunted the animal to near extinction. The otter is now protected, however, and its numbers are steadily climbing. A sea otter at rest, indeed, seems to be the embodiment of serene assurance. Floating on its back in the secure tangle of a kelp bed, it wraps a long ribbon of the plant around its body to anchor it in place as it gently rocks in the rhythm of the ocean.

The rhythm of the tide pervades all of coastal life. And although it creates a fierce presence as it crashes upon solid rock, it has an even greater influence as it spills over a sandy beach. Here, where the land is far more under the dominion of the sea, the unstable setting the sea creates is far less hospitable to wildlife.

Waves crash on the beach thousands of times a day. With each crash, countless bits of sand, rock, and broken shells swirl frantically and are deposited on shore as the wave rushes forward. With each retreat, the water steals away countless other bits of beach. Indeed, the sand itself seems to flow like a sea, and if water doesn't rearrange it, the wind will. Sand that blows out of the reach of high tide helps form dunes that rise behind the beach. Although ever shifting, they are the one place on the immediate beach where plants may gain a roothold.

Bend down and scoop up a handful of sand. Chances are, its grains will consist mostly of quartz, worn from slabs of granite, the rock that makes up most of the earth's crust. The smooth, rounded grains are probably older than those that still retain some angles. The sand may also contain darker flecks of rock such as basalt, once spewed red-hot from a volcano; chalky grains of limestone; pink flecks of feldspar; and the opalescent glow of tiny shell fragments, crushed and burnished in the tumult of the shore. This single handful may contain bits of rock from a prehistoric beach, granite that once crowned a mountaintop, rock that once supported the weight of a dinosaur. Such is the understated history of the sandy shore, where the immediate scenery, from shoreline to sand dunes, may shift from day to day.

Only a few plants and animals are specially adapted to make the sandy shore their permanent home. Unlike the rocky coast, the sandy shore has few large animal visitors. In fact, aside from the presence of shore birds, animal life on the beach usually reveals itself only by the clues it leaves behind.

Close to the water, after the passage of a wave has wetted the sand, tiny holes popping with bubbles mark the burrow of a mole crab. Tiny footprints in the sand record the passage of a small mouse. Much larger prints show that a raccoon and a skunk have visited the beach recently. Small burrows in the dunes reveal the hiding places of insects, and the sand around a larger hole shows the comings and goings of a ghost crab.

This little crab is well adapted to life on the sandy shore and combines characteristics common to many shore animals. Named for its ability to disappear in an instant, it is lightly colored, allowing it to blend with the sand and to absorb as little as possible of the sun's heat. Indeed, the ghost crab may blend in so well with its surroundings that sometimes it is the crab's shadow, rather than the crab itself, that gives it away. To avoid detection, the crab will usually rest with its body flat against the sand so as not to cast a shadow.

Rarely, however, does the ghost crab leave its burrow during the day. When it ventures out at night, it visits the tideline where it scavenges on the dead plants and animals stranded there by the tide. The trip to the water's edge is essential for another reason. Although the ghost crab seems thoroughly at home in the sand dunes, it is still very much a creature of the sea and must wet its gills with ocean water. Every night, the ghost crab becomes a living bridge between the beach and the sea.

142

This strange contrast of marine life in a parched setting is typical of the sandy shore, for the very nature of sand makes desertlike qualities inescapable. Water swiftly percolates through the loosely packed grains, making the sand's upper layers nearly always dry. Its surface, too, grows scorchingly hot in the midday sun. And the ever-shifting sand makes an insecure foundation for plants and animals. The plants that do colonize a dune survive by sending out long underground stems to anchor them or by creeping over the dune's surface, as do two varieties of morning glories, remarkably delicate-looking plants that are found only on coastal sands. Once anchored by plants, the dunes become barriers that shield the life behind them from blowing sand and salt spray, permit more luxuriant plant growth, and help halt ocean flooding during storms.

The heat and the dryness of the beach seem uninviting in contrast with the cool, soothing caress of the ocean's waters. Nonetheless, some ocean creatures routinely forsake sea for land. On the mid-reaches of America's Atlantic Coast, for example, a strange, ancient ritual unfolds, one that began about 150 million years ago, well before most of the rest of the animal life currently populating the earth even existed. In May and

Contoured by winds blowing onto shore, beach dunes rise in front of the Pacific Ocean (left). The near-desert environment of the sandy beach invites few permanent residents. Among the special few: delicate beach morning glories (below) which grow in widespread runners that help stabilize the sand and support the burrows of some small animals; and ghost crabs (right) that leave their sandy tunnels each evening and march to the sea to soak their gills and to feed.

143

The food-rich ocean spreads a varied banquet shared by many shore birds. Once a year, when horseshoe crabs crawl onto Atlantic beaches to mate, gulls congregate in throngs to feed on the eggs and any overturned adults (below). Sanderlings (right) work the beach for any morsels the lapping waves may fortuitously wash up.

June, on nights of peak high tides, thousands upon thousands of horseshoe crabs crawl out of the ocean onto the beach to lay and fertilize their eggs. Most return to the sea with the tides, but many others become stranded on the beach. The spawning of the horseshoes happens to coincide with the arrival of hordes of birds on their migrations to the north. These voyagers conveniently replenish their energy supplies by consuming the horseshoes' eggs and any haplessly stranded adults.

Without a doubt, no group of creatures is more evocative of the seashore than the shore birds. A graceful and raucous presence on most beaches, some birds trot along the shore, skirting each incoming wave to see what tasty morsels it has washed up. Others fly low over

the water, sharp eyes cocked for the shimmer of a fish.

The best-known of these birds are the gulls, largely scavengers of shoreline debris. By feasting on the dead plant and animal matter the waves wash up, they help keep the beach free of refuse. Many other birds also follow the path of the waves with a keen eye and run along the edges like comically hesitant swimmers. The spotted sandpiper, its relative the sanderling, and the tiny snowy plover dart into the wake of receding waves to snatch up small crustaceans and shrimp the waves have flushed from the sand.

Many other birds, not content to wait for the sea to hand them their meal, fly over its surface to snatch small fish from the water. The tern, a member of the gull family, is one such graceful fisherman. One species, the Caspian tern, has fine-polished its technique by flying close to the water's surface with its beak pointed down, apparently so as not to waste a fraction of a second when it spots a fish. The bird instantly dives into the water to snare its prey. It is also known, however, for raiding other birds' nests of eggs and young.

Another sleek fisherman, the black skimmer, has an even more specialized fishing technique. It flies very low over the ocean's surface and drops the lower half of its beak so that it slices the water. When it encounters a small crustacean or fish, the upper half clamps down on it. The bird raises its bill from the water to swallow its prey, and then drops it again to continue fishing—all without breaking the rhythm of its flight.

Virtually all birds that feed along sandy beaches, whatever their lifestyle, have a set of common characteristics that are the mark of their environment. The most influential part of the environment is the flat, level shoreline with few trees and hiding places. Consequently, most shore birds that spend a great deal of time trotting on the ground, such as sandpipers, willets, and plovers, are protectively colored in variations on a general theme of white, brown, gray, and black. Most, too, are ground nesters, which means that the eggs and young must also be protectively colored; no bright white or pastel-hued eggs are found here: Shore birds' eggs are colored and mottled like patches of pebbly sand. Nor is this a place for helpless, closed-eyed, open-beaked, chirping young, which would be hopelessly easy prey. Rather, the young of most beach-dwelling birds emerge from their eggs nearly prepared to fend for themselves. Endowed with a full, downy covering, wide-open eyes, and swift little legs, they can

Black skimmers need not wait for the tides to wash food onto the beach; they harvest their meals directly from the sea. As they slice the sea water with their beaks, they snap up small fish, shrimp, and other meals.

scuttle for shelter very soon after they hatch.

Such well-developed young, however, require quite long incubation periods and large eggs, meaning that shore birds tend to have small broods. Most shore birds lay four eggs, although the Caspian tern lays two or three and the royal tern lays only one. All these birds are watchful parents, swift to fly into the air with a sharp, squawking rebuke for any beachcomber who strolls through their nesting site.

On a few islands off the mainland and on one beach on the California coast, shore birds share their sandy territory with an ungainly creature—the Northern elephant seal, named for the male's distinctive elephantine snout. In November and January, elephant seals haul out to give birth to calves and to breed on these sandy coves. After an evening spent feeding, the elephant seals head for the sandy beach. Like huge grubs, they inch their way out onto the land and then flop down on the sand, where they remain largely motionless for most of the day. The seals flip sand on their backs to protect them from the sun. These large creatures, so well suited to the sea, look oddly at one with the sandy beach.

Walk a short distance from a sandy beach and it is not unusual to encounter a saltwater marsh. But although saltwater marshes often lie next to sandy shores, the contrast between the two worlds is great. Unlike the sandy shore with its relatively sparse plant and animal life, the saltwater marsh brims with life.

Combine the best ingredients that nature has to offer and the result is a world overflowing with productivity. The river brings its load of nutrient-rich waters from the land, and the sea adds nutrients to it at each high tide, making the marsh one of the richest of all habitats.

The origin of the saltwater marsh is similar to that of the freshwater marsh. Like the freshwater marsh, it forms in places where the flow of water is slow enough to allow silt to collect and plants to take root. For the saltwater marsh, these quiet places are usually found in open, shallow bays and behind offshore barriers. The

A day at the beach: A bull elephant seal (far left) tosses a blanket of sand on its back as protection from sunburn. A snowy plover (left) incubates its camouflaged eggs, and a Caspian tern (below) cools its two chicks under the shade of its wings.

arrival of plants increases the marsh's fertility and buffers the tides. Tall, tough salt-marsh grasses predominate here, particularly cordgrass, which with its thick snarl of roots helps collect silt, build turf, and eventually reclaim a portion of the land from the sea.

This tranquil and bountiful place is not without its hardships, however. Unlike in the freshwater marsh, the water level of a saltwater marsh predictably changes twice a day—every time the tide comes in or goes out. The tides, furthermore, constantly alter the marsh's mix of salt and fresh water. The marsh may contain nearly all salt water when the tide flows in, then completely revert to fresh water as the tide goes out. To cope with these fluctuations, most saltwater plants have developed filtration systems that get rid of excess salt. And many animals that live in the salt marsh have developed a tolerance to these changeable conditions.

One plant, the pickleweed, actually stores fresh water within its succulent stems. The pickleweed has an unusual cohort in the salt-marsh harvest mouse. This little creature, found only in the salt marshes around San Francisco Bay, feeds almost exclusively on the bitter pickleweed. The mouse is so well adapted to its brackish-water home that it even drinks salt water.

The saltwater marsh's slow waters and its food-rich mix of salt and fresh water attract numerous and varied creatures which find an ideal home here. Razor clams, soft-shelled clams, and burrowing shrimp live beneath the nutritious muck of the mud flats. Oysters, clams, and blue crabs live on the floor of areas always covered by water. Fiddler crabs and purple crabs live in the mud around the grassy edges approaching the water. The marsh even serves as a nursery for many deep-sea fish. Striped bass, bluefish, and flounder, for example, will spend their vulnerable youth within the protected borders of the salt marshes and swim to the open sea only when they are adults.

The many small lives within the mud become food for many larger creatures. Diamondback terrapins snatch mollusks and shellfish and graze on plants in the eastern salt marshes. And throngs of birds come to harvest the rich food supply. Waders—especially herons and egrets—stroll through the water on their long, stiltlike legs, snatching up small fish and crustaceans that meander past. Ospreys scoop their fish meals with their powerful talons. Flamingos sort their meals from the water with their sievelike bills.

Not coincidentally, one of America's rarest and most wonderful birds continues to battle extinction from within the stronghold of a saltwater marsh. In 1937, the last fifteen whooping cranes in the United States wintered in a saltwater marsh along the coast of Texas.

A salt marsh is one of the most productive habitats on earth. In tidal creeks such as this one on the New Jersey coast (left), ocean water combines with fresh water to create an especially food-rich broth. Diamondback terrapins (far left) lay their eggs in the salt marsh and harvest the snails, crabs, and worms that live in the nutritious mud. The salt harvest mouse of San Francisco Bay (right) grazes on bitter pickleweed and even drinks salt water.

149

Although not completely out of danger, thanks to intense conservation efforts the whooping crane has been rescued from extinction. The crane's Texas wintering grounds are now a protected National Wildlife Refuge, and a second flock has been established in Idaho.

Far to the southeast of the whooping crane's Texas wintering grounds, another coastal setting emerges with a special flavor all its own. Fringing the southern tip of Florida and most of that state's coastal islands lies the tropical counterpart of the saltwater marsh: the tangled, exotic world of the mangrove swamp.

The center of the overflowing life in this coastal world is the mangrove tree itself. On its branches, legions of water birds nest in enormous, raucous rookeries. Herons, egrets, ibis, brown pelicans, and dozens of other kinds of birds find a ready supply of both construction materials and building sites within the snarl of mangrove branches. And because mangrove thickets can grow in areas covered by salt water, these rookeries are isolated from predators like raccoons and snakes.

Among the submerged tips of the mangrove roots and in the rich mud in which they anchor live countless snails, crabs, worms, and other aquatic animals that provide a richly spread dinner table for the birds perching above. Roseate spoonbills swing their broad, flat bills back and forth in the mud searching for shrimp, and wood ibises repeatedly kick the rich muck with their toes, hoping to bring up a tasty, small fish.

Besides providing food and shelter for boisterous multitudes of birds, the mangrove swamp embraces two creatures quietly fighting a battle for survival. In the mangrove-bordered brackish creeks and saltwater bays of southern Florida, the United States's population of the American crocodile makes a last bid against extinction. And in the mangrove swamps on a few of the western Florida Keys, a small population of tiny Key deer has survived the encroachments of civilization.

The American crocodile, a relative of the American alligator, fell prey to hide hunters and to a widespread loss of habitat to development in southern Florida. Although probably never numerous, in the 1950's the American crocodile population dipped to less than 300 individuals. Now, under the protection of the Endangered Species Act, American crocodiles subsist in two tiny breeding populations, one in Everglades National Park and one on Key Largo. No one knows for sure what the current population count is for these spectacular reptiles, but they seem to be holding their own in these

Because mangrove trees can grow in salt water (left), they offer wood ibis, herons, egrets (below), and dozens of other kinds of birds nesting sites inaccessible to land-bound predators.

Framed by a mangrove's flying-buttress root, a pair of Key deer munch on mangrove leaves. The tiny white-tailed deer, found nowhere else in the world, now live in a refuge on one of the Florida Keys.

remote mangrove sanctuaries.

The story of the tiny Key deer is more obviously one of success. In 1949, only 30 of these miniature white-tailed deer were left. Now, thanks to man's concern, the Key deer are slowly making a comeback on a protected refuge. A population of about 400 Key deer threads its way through the mangrove thickets' junglelike mess of branches and prop roots.

It is indeed fitting that these struggles for survival are being played out within America's mangrove swamps. Few living things, plant or animal, battle so hardily against powerful enemies as does the mangrove tree. For despite all its strange, tangled beauty, a mangrove tree is, above all, a survivor.

In the struggles between land and sea, the mangrove emerges as a key figure: The tree helps protect the mainland against the ravages of the sea's fury; it even helps to build land along the coast.

As the sea lashes against the land in powerful waves, the mangroves hold fast. Anchored by their remarkable roots that branch out from the tree like stabilizing flying buttresses, mangrove trees have been known to withstand even the 200-mile-an-hour winds of some Florida hurricanes. In fact, if the mangroves were not there to cushion the land against the hurricanes, the coast of Florida would be dramatically reshaped after each one.

In the thick snarl of submerged mangrove roots, mud and silt constantly accumulate. Gradually, enough soil builds up for the coastline to extend slightly into the ocean. Each autumn a new battalion of seedlings settles farther and farther from the mainland. In time, some of these seedlings will develop into thick stands, mud will collect around their roots, and the land will continue to creep, inch by inch, into the ocean.

In this final frontier of the shore, where the land is buffeted by the worst of the sea's storms, the mangrove emerges as a hero. It is strong enough to fight against a mighty enemy, but generous enough to give sanctuary to the fragile life in nature.

153

INDEX

Illustrations are in **boldface**.

CREDITS

Cover: Steven C. Wilson/ Entheos. **Page 1:** Tom and Pat Leeson. **Pages 2-3:** Steven Fuller/Animals Animals. **Pages 4-5:** Tom and Pat Leeson. **Pages 6-7:** Art Wolfe.

THE MOUNTAINS

Page 9: David Falconer/Bruce Coleman, Inc. **Pages 10-11:** Jeff Gnass. **Page 12:** Jeff Gnass. **Page 13:** Carr Clifton. **Page 14:** Steven Fuller. **Page 15 Top:** W.F. Scott, Jr.; **bottom:** David Muench. **Page 16:** Spencer Swanger/Tom Stack and Assoc. **Pages 16-17:** Keith Gunnar. **Pages 18-19:** David C. Fritts. **Page 20:** Jeff Foott. **Page 21 Left:** Joe McDonald; **right:** Jeff Foott. **Page 22:** John Shaw. **Page 23 Top:** Annie Griffiths/Brandenburg-Griffiths Photography; **middle:** Tom and Pat Leeson; **bottom:** Tom and Pat Leeson. **Pages 24-25:** Jeff Gnass. **Page 25:** Carr Clifton. **Page 26:** Jim Brandenburg/Brandenburg-Griffiths Photography. **Page 27 Top left:** Lynn Rogers; **bottom left:** Stephen J. Krasemann/DRK Photo; **right:** Leonard Lee Rue III/National Audubon Society Collection/Photo Re-

searchers. **Page 28:** William J. Weber. **Page 29:** Bill Ivy. **Page 30:** Art Wolfe. **Page 31 Top:** Thase Daniel; **bottom:** Bruce D. Thomas. **Page 32:** David Cavagnaro. **Page 33 Top:** Larry Ulrich; **bottom:** Joe McDonald/Animals Animals. **Pages 34-35:** Bill Byrne. **Page 36:** Dick Smith. **Page 37:** Brian Milne/First Light Toronto. **Page 38:** Lynn Rogers. **Pages 38-39:** Art Wolfe. **Page 39:** Stephen J. Krasemann/DRK Photo. **Pages 40-41:** Wolfgang Bayer.

THE PRAIRIES

Page 43: Steven C. Wilson/- Entheos. **Pages 44-45:** Robert P. Carr. **Pages 46-47:** David Muench. **Page 47:** Jim Brandenburg/Brandenburg-Griffiths Photography. **Page 48 Top:** Craig Blacklock; **bottom:** Don and Pat Valenti/ Tom Stack and Assoc. **Page 49:** Stephen J. Krase-mann/DRK Photo. **Page 50:** David Muench. **Page 51:** Ox-ford Scientific Films/Animals Animals. **Page 52 Left:** Tom J. Ulrich. **Pages 52-53:** Lynn M. Stone. **Page 53 Top:** John Shaw; **bottom right:** Robert L. Dunne. **Page 54:** Ernest Wilkinson/Animals Animals. **Page 55:** Gary R. Zahm. **Page 56:** Gary R. Zahm. **Page 57:** Don Cornelius. **Pages 58-59:** Charles Krebs. **Page 60:** Len Rue, Jr./Animals Animals. **Page 61:** Don and Pat Valenti/Tom Stack and Assoc. **Page 62:** © Walt Disney Productions.

Page 63 Top: Franz J. Camenzind; **bottom:** Jerry L. Ferrara. **Page 64:** Franz J. Camenzind. **Page 65:** Brian Milne/First Light Toronto. **Pages 66-67:** L. Joseph Neibauer.

THE DESERTS

Page 69: Peter Kresan. **Pages 70-71:** Jerry Sieve. **Pages 72-73:** Larry Ulrich. **Page 74:** © David Muench. **Page 75 Top:** Dr. E.R. Degginger; **bottom:** Bruce D. Thomas. **Page 76:** C. Allan Morgan. **Pages 76-77:** © David Muench. **Page 78:** Jeff Gnass. **Page 79:** Larry R. Ditto/Tom Stack and Assoc. **Page 80:** Fiona Sunquist/Tom Stack and Assoc. **Pages 80-81:** Stouffer Enterprises, Inc./- Animals Animals. **Page 81:** John Shaw. **Page 82:** James Tallon. **Page 83 Top:** George H. Harrison; **bottom:** Karl Maslowski. **Page 84:** Peter Kresan. **Pages 84-85:** Wolf-gang Bayer. **Page 86 Left:** Rick McIntyre; **right:** Willis Peterson. **Page 87:** Jerry Sieve. **Page 88 Left:** Dr. E.R. Degginger; **right:** Joe DiStefano/National Audubon Society Collection/Photo Re-searchers. **Page 89:** C. Allan Morgan. **Page 90 Top:** Leonard Lee Rue III/National Audubon Society Collection/- Photo Researchers; **bottom:** Erwin and Peggy Bauer. **Page 91:** William J. Weber. **Pages 92-93:** Peter Kresan. **Page 93 Top:** Peter Kresan; **bottom:** Peter Kresan. **Page 94 Left:**

David Cavagnaro; **right:** Wil-lard Clay. **Page 95 Left:** Robert P. Carr; **right:** Andreé Robinson. **Pages 96-97:** Jeff Gnass.

THE WETLANDS

Page 99: Jeff Foott. **Pages 100-101:** Wendell Metzen. **Page 102:** John Shaw. **Page 103:** © 84 Frans Lanting. **Page 104:** Milton Rand/Tom Stack and Assoc. **Page 105:** Caulion Singletary. **Page 106 Left:** John Shaw; **top right:** Robert W. Mitchell/Tom Stack and Assoc. **bottom right:** Dr. Wm. M. Harlow. **Page 107 Top:** Jack Dermid; **bottom:** Breck P. Kent. **Page 108 Left:** Dwight Kuhn; **right:** Rod Planck/Tom Stack and Assoc. **Page 109:** Johnny Johnson. **Page 110-111:** Tupper Ansel Blake. **Page 112 Left:** Lynn Rogers; **right:** Gary Meszaros. **Page 113 Top:** Lynn Rogers; **bottom:** Jeff Foott. **Page 114:** George H. Harrison. **Page 115 Left:** John Shaw; **right:** Tim Fitzharris. **Page 116:** Dr. E.R. Degginger. **Page 117 Top:** Bill Byrne; **bottom:** Robert Noonan. **Pages 118-119:** Joseph Van Wormer/ Bruce Coleman, Inc. **Page 120 Top:** Larry West; **bot-tom:** Walter Dawn. **Page 121 Left:** Tom Bledsoe/National Audubon Society Collection/ Photo Researchers; **right:** C.C. Lockwood. **Page 122 Top:** Dr. E.R. Degginger. **Pages 122-123:** Wendell Metzen. **Page 123 Top:** John Shaw.

Pages 124-125: C.C. Lockwood.

THE COASTS

Page 127: Philip Hyde. **Pages 128-129:** Larry Ulrich. **Page 130:** Jeff Gnass. **Page 131:** Frank S. Balthis. **Page 132:** Lynn M. Stone. **Page 133:** Victor B. Scheffer. **Page 134:** Willard Clay. **Page 135 Top:** Jeff Foott/Bruce Coleman, Inc.; **bottom:** Breck P. Kent. **Page 136:** W.E. Townsend, Jr. **Page 137:** Jeff Foott. **Page 138 Left:** Bob and Clara Calhoun/ Bruce Coleman, Inc.; **right:** Jeff Foott. **Page 139 Top:** Betty Randall; **bottom:** Jeff Foott. **Pages 140-141:** Jeff Foott. **Page 142:** Charles A. Mauzy. **Page 143 Left:** Lynn M. Stone; **right:** Stephen J. Krasemann/DRK Photo. **Page 144 Top:** Jeff Foott; **bottom:** Zig Leszczynski/Animals Animals. **Page 145:** Steven C. Wilson/ Entheos. **Page 146:** © 84 Frans Lanting. **Page 147 Top:** M.P. Kahl; **bottom:** Jeff Foott. **Page 148 Left:** Jack Dermid. **Pages 148-149:** Michael Gallagher/Bruce Coleman, Inc. **Page 149:** Jeff Foott. **Page 150:** Jerry Sieve. **Page 151:** Stan Osolinski. **Pages 152-153:** C.C. Lockwood/Bruce Coleman, Inc.

Library of Congress
Cataloging in
Publication Data

Jensen, Karen, 1957-
    America, land of wildlife.

    Includes index.
    1. Biotic communities—United States. 2. Natural history—United States. I. National Wildlife Federation. II. Title.
    QH104.J46   1984   574.5'0973
    ISBN 0-912186-55-0   84-600258

NATIONAL WILDLIFE FEDERATION

Dr. Jay D. Hair
Executive Vice President

James D. Davis
*Senior Vice President,
Membership Development
and Publications*

STAFF FOR THIS BOOK

Howard F. Robinson
Managing Editor

Cecilia I. Parker
Editor

Donna Miller
Design Director

Laura B. Ackerman
Research Editor

Dr. Raymond E. Johnson
Wildlife Consultant

Donna J. Reynolds
Editorial Assistant

Priscilla Sharpless
Production and Printing

Margaret E. Wolf
Permissions Editor

Tina Isom
Pam McCoy
Production Artists

Michael E. Loomis
Production Coordinator

NATIONAL WILDLIFE FEDERATION
1412 Sixteenth Street, N.W., Washington, D.C. 20036